DELICATE DEBATES ON ISLAM

DELICATE DEBATES ON ISLAM

Policymakers and Academics Speaking
with Each Other

Edited by

Jan Michiel Otto and Hannah Mason

Leiden University Press

The publication of this book has been made possible by a grant from LUCIS, the Leiden University Centre for the Study of Islam & Society.

Cover design: Tarek Atrissi Design
Layout: The DocWorkers, Almere

ISBN   978 90 8728 117 5
e-ISBN   978 94 0060 036 2
NUR   717 / 820

Contents

Foreword: About LUCIS

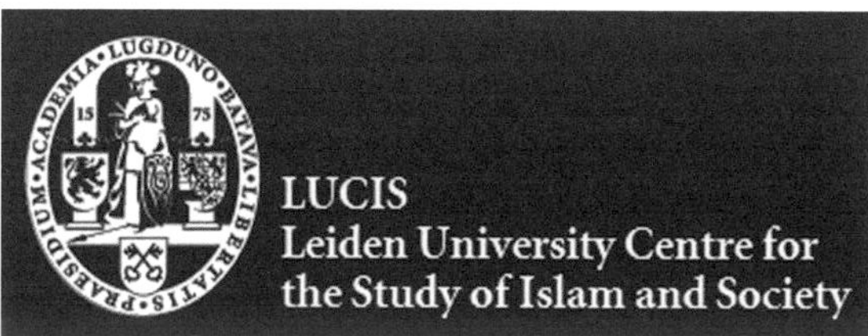

Delicate Debates on Islam reflects and elaborates on the proceedings of the official inaugural conference of the Leiden Centre for the Study of Islam and Society (LUCIS), held on 14 October 2009 in the 'Academiegebouw' in Leiden, themed 'Islam: Academia & Policy'. The book includes both the speeches held on that day, as well as a number of related contributions.

The Leiden University Centre for the Study of Islam and Society was established on 1 January 2009 as a multidisciplinary and interfaculty centre of expertise of Leiden University in the area of Islam and Muslim societies. LUCIS joins academics from the Leiden Faculties of Humanities, Law and the Social Sciences. By means of lectures and symposia LUCIS aims to share ongoing research in the area of Islam and Muslim societies with colleagues and other interested parties and to promote the exchange of knowledge between academics.

LUCIS wishes to provide an answer to the public demand for knowledge in the area of Islam and Muslims societies by organising public lectures and debates. Moreover, LUCIS coordinates courses, research and other activities on request of public or civil society organisations.

LUCIS aims to bring together and promote all educational courses in the area of Islam. Through the online catalogue 'Study of Islam' on the LUCIS website, the institute provides an overview of all modules in the area of Islam and Muslim societies. http://www.hum.leidenuniv.nl/lucis/onderwijs/onderwijsportal-islamstudies.html. LUCIS also invites guest lecturers to speak about their specific areas of expertise.

Delicate Debates on Islam. Policymakers and Academics Speaking with Each Other: an Introduction

Jan Michiel Otto and Hannah Mason

Politics, Polarisation, Populism

Since the late 1990s, Islam has moved up the political agenda to become one of the most controversial issues in Dutch society. Whereas Islam used to be considered as a world religion with its own norms and values in the same way as any other religion, several politicians and public figures have started resorting to Islam as a way of explaining the major problems in society. Ayaan Hirsi Ali[1] and Pim Fortuyn[2] called the religion 'backward'; Theo van Gogh[3] wrote repeatedly about Moroccan immigrant Muslims as 'the goatfuckers' or the 'fifth column'. Fortuyn was shot by a radical animal rights activist in 2002, just before his right-wing party was about to gain significant support in the upcoming elections. Van Gogh was brutally murdered by a Moroccan fundamentalist in 2004, and Hirsi Ali moved to the United States in 2006, where she joined a neoconservative think tank. The heated atmosphere in the Netherlands during the years after 9/11 has been captured well by Ian Buruma in his book *Murder in Amsterdam*.[4] More recently, the anti-Islam debate has gained momentum again through the one-liners of the parliamentarian Geert Wilders, leader of the populist 'Party of Freedom' (PVV). The plain language employed by the PVV has urged people to speak out for or against Islam, which has aggravated the polarisation of society. In the 2010 elections, Wilders' party secured 24 seats in parliament, which enabled him to join a centre-right minority government without having to take political responsibility and allowing him to veto any policy he does not like.[5] Combined with large-scale migration and financial instability, the political climate in the Netherlands has changed from one of tolerance and stability to suspicion, dissatisfaction and unrest.

The Netherlands does not seem to be the only European country where strong anti-Islam voices are being heard. In October 2010, the

German Chancellor Angela Merkel announced publicly that she believed that the concept of a multicultural society had died its death.[6] This was preceded by the departure of one of the board members of the Central Bank of Germany, Thilo Sarrazin, in September 2010 after an extremely discriminatory statement about the Muslim population in Germany.[7] More recently,[8] the UK's prime minister David Cameron spoke about the failure of 'state multiculturalism', calling it a cause for radicalisation of young Muslims. In France, an opinion poll carried out by the Harris Institute in March 2011 for *Le Parisien* newspaper revealed that the right-wing and anti-Islam politician Marine Le Pen would win 23% of the votes (thereby surpassing the current President Nicolas Sarkozy).[9]

This growing amount of attention on Islam has been picked up by the European media, which tends to extract the most sensational aspects of developments around the world. Certainly, some quality newspapers try to present a balanced picture, but generally speaking there seems to be an uneven interest in and focus on problems in the Muslim world or in the West which can be ascribed to Muslims or Islam. In this sense mass media plays into the ideas of populist thinkers such as Wilders and Le Pen. Moreover, following Kapuscinski, 'even if we assume that they lie, [mass media] still have an enormous effect on us, because they establish the list of our topics, thus limiting our field of thinking to information and opinions that decision makers themselves have chosen and defined.'[10]

Academics in Search of an Audience?

In this highly polarised climate and among the many one-sided views presented by influential politicians and media, policymakers are pressed for answers on serious questions about Islam and Muslims. Therefore the need for unbiased research-based information seems more pertinent than ever. This book will explore ways in which academics can contribute to or are already influencing the debate and assist policymakers in answering questions and making decisions.

There is nothing new in the idea that scholars and policymakers need to better inform one another. Nor in the challenge for academics to step down from their ivory tower and make their work more accessible to the public. As John Esposito states in this book: 'Academics and academic centres have a critical role to play in the formulation of government policies and international relations.' More interesting is the question of *how* academics can get more involved in the public debate on Islam and Muslims. This question derives mainly from the common accusation that academics, including those who study Islam and Muslims, write in too abstract terms, with an excessive eye for detail, or even incomprehensibly. Who would want to read a book about the incorporation of sharia, when the first paragraph states that the concept of sharia itself has four different meanings?[11] Pressed for time, politicians, government officials and journalists seem to prefer summaries, abstracts, or fact sheets over elaborate books and reports. There are many who argue that this is one of the main reasons why academic knowledge does not filter through to public opinion.

In the present context writings on Islam and Muslims that academics may offer to the public also deserve scrutiny, as academia reflects a polarisation of opinions similar to what we see in politics and society. In the body of international academic knowledge on Islam and Muslims we can distinguish two competing perspectives. Whilst the first view, known as essentialism, considers the Islamic religious sources as representing the essence of 'the Islamic civilisation', 'the Islamic culture' and 'the Islamic legal system', the second perspective, which has been labelled pluralism or multiplism, takes the variety of countries and social contexts in which such norms are actually formulated, interpreted and applied in real life as its point of departure.[12] Whereas the majority of scholars, including the authors of this book, are not impressed by the academic qualities of most essentialist writings, populist politicians seem to find this point of view highly attractive.

The orientation and outcomes of scholarly work on Islam and Muslims may also be determined, or at least restricted, by its academic discipline. To illustrate the point, one could take the example of the controversial punishment of stoning. If you are a theologist, an islamologist, or an expert in interpreting traditions (*hadith*) as a major textual source of Islamic norms, you may come to the conclusion that stoning as a sentence for adultery is prescribed. However, if you are a legal scholar, looking at national legislation and case law in Islamic countries, you may conclude that most Muslim countries have not incorporated such Islamic norms in their national laws. A socio-legal scholar may note that in countries which prescribe stoning as a punishment, even if in exceptional cases the judges pronounce such sentence, in most Muslim countries it is just not carried out. An anthropologist may observe that local communities sometimes try to legitimise their customary 'mob justice' with references to sharia and a so-called Islamic court. As a political scientist one may see that the sanction of stoning is being used by politicians as a tool to install fear among opponents, or to fight social evils such as prostitution, drinking and drug addiction. The sociologist may observe that opinions about this sanction amongst the people are widely diverse. In sum, it appears that the type of questions asked and the types of sources used can have a significant impact on the conclusions drawn.

This potentially leads to a situation, in which politicians will seek advice from those experts whose opinions fit their political convictions. For example, there is one professor of Islamic studies in the Netherlands whose scholarship is usually invoked to support statements criticising Islam and Muslims. Dr Johannes (Hans) Jansen, a retired professor at Utrecht University, who often appears in the media, used to be cited by Ayaan Hirsi Ali and has given testimony during the court case against Geert Wilders for inciting hatred against Muslims in 2010. He verified statements, which Wilders made about Islam by reference to verses of the Qur'an. However, prominent professors in Qur'anic studies and Islamic law, Dr Fred Leemhuis of Groningen University and Dr Rudolph Peters of Amsterdam University respectively, on the basis of their studies and interpretations have come to conclusions diametrically opposed to Jansen's views.

Policymakers in Search of Relevant Knowledge

It is therefore not surprising that policymakers have trouble finding their way in the complex web of contrasting academic ideas about Islam and Muslims. This book starts with some of the questions that policymakers are faced with and to which an academic response is sought. Job Cohen introduces some of the most fundamental questions, derived from experiences gained during his nine-year term as Mayor of Amsterdam (2001-2010). In the first chapter, he asks 'the academics' to what extent the following assumptions are correct: whether Islam is a violent religion, whether the Netherlands on the whole is 'islamising', whether the number of followers of the more extreme variants of Islam is increasing, and whether Islam is a stagnant and backwards religion. Moreover, he is interested in the compatibility between Islam and democracy. He asks the researchers of Islam and Muslim societies to provide him and other policymakers with useful insights into relevant developments in the countries of origin of Muslim immigrants and into their needs and problems in the Netherlands, which would help making more effective policy in the Netherlands.

Whilst Cohen draws attention to national policy problems, Jaap de Hoop Scheffer considers, in the second chapter of this book, a few of the dilemma's he was confronted with during his term as Secretary General of NATO. It appears that NATO has found itself increasingly in conflict areas in the Muslim world, notably in Afghanistan, Iraq and more recently in Libya. He touches on the benefits and problems of a foreign policy which connects issues of defence, diplomacy and development. He also raises issues of universal norms and values and wonders whether it is possible for any country to be, what he calls, 'normative neutral' by referring to the universal declaration of human rights.

De Hoop Scheffer, too, asks 'the academics' whether they can shed some light on what in the Muslim world can be ascribed to culture and what to religion. He feels that there is a need for greater knowledge about Islam in the West and appeals to LUCIS to engage in this question.

Nikolaos van Dam, who served the Dutch Ministry of Foreign Affairs as ambassador in Baghdad, Cairo, Ankara and Jakarta, considers the contributions that academics may be able to provide to policymakers. Drawing on a number of cases he encountered during his career, Van Dam, a scholar of Arabic, Islam and Muslim societies himself, gives an inside view of how this works out in the actual operations of the Dutch Ministry of Foreign Affairs. His chapter recognises the potential value of academic research, but also signals the difficulties in making scholarly work relevant in the day-to-day activities of the foreign office. He points to deficiencies within the ministry, where specialist knowledge is neither encouraged nor used as it could be and, in his view, should be done. He regards the relationship between researcher and policymaker as an inherently complex one. By focusing on the opportunities and constraints of both diplomats and other government officials, as well as researchers, he concludes with some suggestions.

Since 1972, the Scientific Council for Government Policy (Wetenschappelijke Raad voor het Regeringsbeleid, WRR), a prominent Dutch public think tank, has played an important role in the dynamic interplay between policy, academic research, public opinion and politics in the Netherlands. The Dutch government is legally obliged to respond officially and formulate its own opinions on matters raised by WRR reports. From 2003-2006, the WRR conducted a major study on whether Islamic activism could offer reference points for democracy and human rights.[13] The WRR's report, published in April 2006, did indeed note a number of important positive reference points, and understandably the report and its underlying studies were hotly debated in the media. Only in July 2007, was the official cabinet response published, after an unusually long period of political and interdepartmental deliberations. As the official response is in fact the only document representing the view of the Dutch government on Islam and its role in the government's policy, the editors have chosen to include some excerpts of an edited translation in this book.[14] The WRR's director Wendy Asbeek Brusse, who was involved in this Islam study as a senior researcher, considers in her contribution some of the necessary conditions for the successful use of academic knowledge by policymakers. She emphasises the need for academics, as well as policymakers, to be aware of the 'logic' of media and politics. Timing, repetition and accessibility are crucial factors.

 The Leiden Propositions on Islam and the Themes of this Book

The four contributions by policymakers and policy advisors mentioned above, raise a wealth of issues and questions that the following articles by academic authors try to address. In order to respond to the accusation that academics are, generally speaking, incapable of offering concise information, the academic authors were also asked to present a small number of short statements or propositions around the theme of Islam and Muslim communities. These can be found as the Leiden Propositions on Islam and Society Studies at the end of this introductory chapter.

An important theme, shared by several of the authors of this book, is the idea that in the Netherlands, as well as in many other Western countries, the public debate hinges too much on Islam. Islam is blamed and regarded as the cause for societal problems too often and unjustifiably so. Asbeek Brusse therefore states that 'academics should contribute towards de-religionising public and political discussions on integration of migrants in the Netherlands'. Maurits Berger presents a similar statement: 'In the process of trying to understand particular Muslim customs or behaviour, people often resort to theological explanations. This approach is one-dimensional and merely contributes towards creating a thwarted image of Muslims.'

A related issue which has been receiving growing attention over the last decade is the connection of religion with terrorism and violence. The idea that certain interpretations of Islam lead to violence is nothing new; evidence can be found throughout history. For centuries radical forms of religion have posed a dilemma to governments, who do their ultimate best to fight terrorism. In the process they have resorted to extreme repression and torture. In turn, such measures are often criticised by the West. This leads to a complex situation in which all pious Muslims become distrusted in the West, whilst they are also desperately needed as advisors and informants for governments.

Not only the public debate, but also academic research needs to be separated from the realm of belief. An important point, which Petra Sijpesteijn makes in her contribution to this book, is that 'the origin and development of Islam can be studied in historical and academic research without calling Islamic beliefs into question.' She hereby emphasises the objectivity and independence of academic research.

A related question that this book is concerned with is 'What is Islam?'. The most important point in relation to this question is the joined emphasis on the diversity of and within Islam. Léon Buskens states in his contribution that 'terms such as "the Islam" and "the Muslim" are merely devout ideals, which are not suitable as analytical concepts. In other words, these terms do not clarify anything. An essence of Islam cannot be determined empirically. In reality Muslims differ in their interpretations of Islam, depending on place, time and personal conditions and convictions. This notion of diversity needs to be the starting point for the undertaking of empirical research and/or policymaking.' Moreover, for policymakers, it is important to realise that 'opinions of the traditional Islamic legal scholars about "The Will of God" according to which Muslims should live, are structured by a number of fundamental inequalities, such as the oppositions between men and women, Muslims and non-Muslims, free men and slaves. Current debates amongst Muslims concern the meaning of these norms in contemporary society and display a wide variety of interpretations, ranging from extremely radical to quite liberal.' Thus, what many people in the West perceive as one ideology with one normative system, in fact consists of a wide range of interpretations and ideas. This is important for policymakers because it means that any Islam-related policy will need to consider the heterogeneity of Muslim communities within a given context.

Related to the argument of recognising diversity, Sijpesteijn gives the historical perspective of this same idea. As a professor of the Arabic language right from the origins of its existence, she looks at the developments of Islam through the centuries and recognises that 'there is no pure early Islam, but rather a multitude of opinions and interpretations about how the first Islamic religious community was organised; the puritan understanding is merely one out of many.' To address the assumption that Islam is stagnant and therefore backwards, as many seem to believe, she states, 'the Western world can benefit from understanding that within Islam there has always been a widely discussed and published diversity, and from the notion that Muslim communities have never been monolithic.'

With Dalia Mogahed and John Esposito present, attention was given to the importance of listening to the voices of mainstream Muslims. Their book *Who Speaks for Islam?*, based on the result of a worldwide Gallup poll had already been brought up by Cohen as a useful resource for policymakers. Esposito notes that it is important to remember that 'Muslims and non-Muslims share common values, concerns and interests.'[15] This is once again confirmed by Mogahed: 'When respondents [of the Gallup poll] were asked to describe their dream for the future, we did not hear about waging jihad, but instead we heard about getting a better job, better economic well-being and prosperity and offering a better future to their children.' Berger makes a similar observation: 'The fact that Muslims wish to incorporate their Islamic lifestyle into Western society is not necessarily incompatible with integration', pointing at the idea that the ideals of the average Muslim in the West does not need to diverge from the local normative system.[16] Jan Michiel Otto points to modernist and liberal Islamic thought by saying that 'the sharia, as interpreted by pious and moderate Muslim scholars such as Khaled Abu el Fadl, Abdullahi An-Naim and the late Nurcholis Madjid, forms a useful source of inspiration for the promotion of human rights and the rule of law.' Politics and public opinion could certainly benefit from an extension and intensification of the communication between such moderate Muslims and Western academics and policymakers.

To follow trends within the Muslim world itself is regarded as an essential task for academics and foreign policy officials alike. Otto, referring to research done into the legal systems of a cross-sample of twelve Muslim countries concludes that 'while the legal systems of most Muslim countries are fairly moderate when it comes to Islam and sharia, their constitutions are actually built on a dual foundation: the rule of law and the tenets of Islam. This ambiguity legitimises the state, the law and the regime as well as the clergy, and it contributes to their peaceful coexistence. However, sometimes this ambiguity leaves the rule of law in a vulnerable position, failing to channel religious-political tensions.' 'The research seems to show that on the whole these countries in terms of women's rights, corporal punishment and democratisation have become more liberal over the last twenty years, and not, as many may have expected, more Islamic in a puritan sense.' Buskens confirms this point: 'Research into the development of the Moroccan legal system shows that the substance of Islamic law has been marginalised over the last century, whilst references to the sharia in the political debate have increased over the last forty years.' Over the last decade references to human rights and democracy have also increased in political debates throughout the Muslim world.

It seems that such longitudinal trends are not often followed or discussed by mass media in the West. The press rather pays attention to the manifestation of anti-Muslim rhetoric, for example in the Netherlands when Wilders launched the idea that all Muslims would be practising *takiyya*, which suggests that Muslims are supposed to hide their true intentions. Berger demonstrates in his contribution how an academic may effectively counter such an accusation by disseminating research-based information amongst the public.

Managing perceptions and expectations about Muslims can be an important task for policymakers. Populists like Wilders and academics like Jansen have succeeded in contributing to feelings of fear and suspicion among the wider public in the Netherlands that 'the sharia' may be introduced as the overarching system. In his contribution Buskens also draws attention to this sentiment of fear, which has resulted from a certain level of ignorance about Islam and Muslims, as well as about law.

Berger states that 'the liberties of the Netherlands allow Muslims to live according to the "sharia", as long as they do so within the framework of national law.' As the official response of the cabinet to the 2006 WRR report notes: 'The cabinet [in the Netherlands] cannot support legal pluralism, meaning the equal co-existence of heterogeneous legal systems. This is evident in the case of administrative and criminal law, as these deal with the relation between state and citizen, and the state does not discriminate between types of citizens. In the case of civil law, and particular the law of obligation, personal status and family law, there is no reason for such legal pluralism. The Dutch state maintains the principle that everyone who resides in the Netherlands should have as much opportunity as possible to organise his/her own life in the way he/she wishes. [...] The cabinet, therefore, aims to offer spaces in its law and policy for traditions which, though they do not belong to the national heritage, are in themselves, not in conflict with basic principles.'

Tensions and trends in European countries such as the Netherlands are of course narrowly linked with developments in the international arena. Esposito remarks that 'the Bush-Blair legacy has made the world less safe, less free.' His contribution exposes the weaknesses of recent foreign policies, both in the West as in the Muslim world. Reflecting on the political decisions of the Western allies is as important as reviewing those of Muslim governments. Esposito also draws on the importance of perceptions. Whilst the Bush administration depicted certain Middle Eastern countries as the axis of evil, the Muslim world has witnessed the double standards it was applying, for example through the events in Guantanamo Bay and Abu Ghraib, but also the critical approach to Hamas after its democratic victory in the 2006 elections in Palestine. Fareed Zakaria refers to the problem in *The Future of Freedom* as 'the Islamic exception'.[17] Esposito calls for a joint effort and a process of constructive engagement, in which both Muslim and non-Muslim countries will need to be prepared to listen to each other.

Having shown some of the various academic responses to discussions around Islam and Muslims, we return to the question of how scholars can be better drawn into the public debate. In the case of the Netherlands, the 2006 WRR report on Islamic activism and the following public debate suggest that not all efforts of scholars to influence policy are fruitless. The official response of the cabinet in 2007 to the report presents a rather balanced and nuanced picture. Some key sections of this document are included in this collection of essays. The excerpts illustrate that the 2007 cabinet recognised the diversity within Islam and did not believe that Islam and democracy or human rights are incompatible. Whilst it supported freedom of religion, it drew the line at violence. And whilst it rejected legal parallelism, it made clear that the Dutch legal system left ample room for people to lead their lives as they wish. However, as Asbeek Brusse notes, 'the times that academic research automatically earned authority in society are over. If academics and policymakers wish to have influence, they will have to understand the dynamics behind media and politics.' The official cabinet response itself received hardly any media attention after Wilders had succeeded to divert the agenda of the parliamentary session in which the response was supposed to be discussed. This illustrates the importance of one of the tasks of academics in this field, i.e. addressing the media and politicians directly and thereby presenting a more truthful and research-based picture of Islam and Muslims.

As this introduction shows, it may be more appropriate to speak of debates rather than one single debate about Islam. The debates take place in a variety of spaces: within and between the West and the Muslim world, within and between countries, amongst and between politicians and other policymakers, academics and journalists, within ministries, universities and media outlets. The debates have become delicate because they deal with issues of national identity, heritage and tradition. The editors of this book believe that this debate deserves in the first place to be based on a balanced account of facts and figures. They also think that these delicate debates should be held in a civilised manner and avoid unnecessary insult or offence.

LEIDEN PROPOSITIONS on the **STUDY** of **ISLAM** and **MUSLIM SOCIETIES** (elaborated in this book)

1. Academics and academic centres have a critical role to play in the formulation of government policies and international relations. (JE)

2. The times that academic research automatically earned authority in society are over. If academics and policymakers wish to have influence on the debates [on Islam], they will have to understand the dynamics behind media and politics. (WAB)

3. Research-based knowledge about 'the Islam' continues to be of utmost importance for public debate, policymaking and politics. (WAB)

4. Academics should contribute towards de-religionising public and political discussions on integration of migrants in the Netherlands. (WAB)

5. There is no pure early Islam, but rather a multitude of opinions and interpretations about how the first Islamic religious community had to be organised; the puritan understanding is merely one out of many. (PS)

6. The origin and development of Islam can be studied in historical and academic research without calling Islamic beliefs into question. (PS)

7. The Western world can benefit from understanding that within Islam there has always been a widely discussed and published diversity, and from the notion that Muslim communities have never been monolithic. (PS)

8. Terms such as 'the Islam' and 'the Muslim' are merely devout ideals, which are not suitable as analytical concepts. In other words, these terms do not clarify anything. The essence of Islam cannot be determined empirically. In reality Muslims differ in their interpretations of the word Islam, depending on place and time. This notion of diversity needs to be the starting point for the undertaking of empirical research and/or policymaking. (LB)

9. Opinions of the traditional Islamic legal scholars about 'The Will of God' according to which Muslims should live, are structured by a number of fundamental inequalities, such as the oppositions between men and women, Muslims and non-Muslims, free men and slaves. Current debates amongst Muslims concern the meaning of these norms in contemporary society and display a wide variety of interpretations, ranging from extremely radical to quite liberal. (LB)

10. Research into the legal systems of a cross-sample of twelve Muslim countries shows that on the whole these countries in terms of women's rights, corporal punishment and democratisation have become more liberal over the last twenty years, and not, as many may have expected, more Islamic in a puritan sense. (JMO)

11. While the legal systems of most Muslim countries are fairly moderate when it comes to Islam and sharia, their constitutions are actually built on a dual foundation: the rule of law and the Islam. This ambiguity legitimises the state, the law and the regime as well as the clergy, and it contributes to their peaceful coexistence. However, sometimes this ambiguity leaves the rule of law in a

vulnerable position, failing to channel religious-political tensions. (JMO)

12. The sharia, as interpreted by pious and moderate Muslim scholars such as Khaled Abu el Fadl, Abdullahi An-Naim and the late Nurcholis Madjid, forms a useful source of inspiration for the promotion of human rights and the rule of law. (JMO)

13. Research into the development of the Moroccan legal system shows that the substance of Islamic law has been marginalised over the last century, whilst references to the sharia in the political debate have increased over the last forty years. This trend seems to occur in other Muslim countries too. These observations go against the commonly accepted idea that the sharia is experiencing a global expansion. (LB)

14. Muslims and non-Muslims share common values, concerns and interests. (JE)

15. Both religious and secular fundamentalists need to redefine their notions of the relationship of religion and the state and the nature and scope of pluralism and tolerance. (JE)

16. The fact that Muslims wish to incorporate their Islamic lifestyle into Western society is not necessarily incompatible with integration. (MB)

17. In the process of trying to understand particular Muslim customs or behaviour, people often resort to theological explanations. This approach is one-dimensional and merely contributes towards creating a thwarted image of Muslims. (MB)

18. The liberties of the Netherlands allow Muslims to live according to the sharia, as long as they do so within the framework of national law. (MB)

19. The Bush-Blair legacy has made the world less safe, less free. (JE)

Notes

1   Ayaan Hirsi Ali is a Dutch feminist activist, politician and founder of the women's rights organisation AGA Foundation. Anno 2011, she is resident in the United States and works as a fellow at the American Enterprise Institute.

2   Pim Fortuyn was a Dutch politician, sociologist, author and columnist (1948-2002).

3   Theo van Gogh was a Dutch film director, script writer and columnist (1957-2004).

4   Ian Buruma, *Murder in Amsterdam. The Death of Theo van Gogh and the Limits of Tolerance* (London: Atlantic Books; 2006).

5   After the 2010 elections, the coalition of the centre party Christian Democrats (CDA) and right-wing Liberals (VVD) needed a third party to secure the majority in the cabinet. They found their partner in Geert Wilders' Freedom Party (PVV), with whom they agreed on most provisions apart from the approach to Islam. The former two parties consider it a religion, whilst the latter calls it a political ideology. The result is a minority coalition under the leadership of Prime Minister Mark Rutte (VVD) with the VVD and the CDA supported on budget and confidence motions by the PVV.

6   'WeltOnline 18/10/2010: www.welt.de/print/welt_kompakt/print_politik/article1-0366 134/Merkel-Multikulti-ist-gescheitert.html (accessed 14 December 2010).

7   He is quoted as saying that Muslims in Germany were sapping the country's intellectual and economic strength and that 'all Jews share the same gene'. www.guardian.co.uk, 02 September 2010: www.guardian.co.uk/world/2010/sep/02/germany-central-bank-decide-sack-thilo-sarrazin (accessed 14 December 2010).

8   BBC Online 05 February 2011: www.bbc.co.uk/news/uk-politics-12371994 (accessed 27 April 2011).

9   Le Parisien.fr 05 March 2011: www.leparisien.fr/election-presidentielle-2012/sondage-presidentielle-marine-le-pen-en-tete-au-premier-tour-05-03-2011-1344656.php (accessed 27 April 2011).

10 'Mass media, even if we don't believe them, if we assume that they lie, still have an enormous effect on us because they establish the list of our topics, thus limiting our field of thinking to information and opinions that decision makers themselves have chosen and defined. After some time, without even being aware of it, we are thinking about the issues that the decision makers want us to think about (usually trivial points exaggerated on purpose, or misrepresented problems). That's why he, who believes he thinks independently, because he is critical of the content served to him by mass media – is mistaken.' From Ryszard Kapuscinski *Lapidarium I: A Selection* (translated by Andrzej Duszenko; 1990, 45-46), http://duszenko.northern.edu/lapidarium/index.html (accessed 15 June 2011).

11 Jan Michiel Otto (ed.), *Sharia incorporated: A Comparative Overview of the Legal Systems of Twelve Muslim Countries in Past and Present* (Leiden: Leiden University Press; 2010).

12 See also Jan Michiel Otto's article 'The compatibility of *sharia* with the rule of law. Fundamental conflict: between civilisations? Within civilisations? Or between scholars?', in In A. 't Groen et al., *Knowledge in Ferment: Dilemmas in Science, Scholarship and Society* (Leiden: Leiden University Press; 2007).

13 Wetenschappelijke Raad for het Regeringsbeleid, *Dynamiek in islamitisch activisme: aanknopingspunten voor democratisering and mensenrechten* (Amsterdam: Amsterdam University Press; 2006). The report was also published in English: WRR (Scientific Council for Government Policy), *Dynamism in Islamic Activism. Reference Points for Democratization and Human Rights* (Amsterdam: Amsterdam University Press; 2006).

14 The 2007 response was presented during the fourth cabinet under Prime Minister Jan Peter Balkenende (2007-2010), which consisted of a coalition of the Christian Democratic Party (CDA), the Labour Party (PvdA) and a moderate Protestant Party (CU). This cabinet was succeeded by a minority government in 2010 (see note 4).

15 John Esposito & Dalia Mogahed's *Who Speaks for Islam? What a billion Muslims really think, Based on Gallup's World Poll – the largest study of its kind* (New York: Gallup Press; 2007) and specifically the methodology of distinguishing between radical and moderate Muslims used by Gallup in their survey amongst Muslims all over the world, was heavily criticised by the Dutch journalist Amanda Kluveld in the

national newspaper *De Volkskrant* of 16 October 2009 (http://opinie.volkskrant.nl/ artikel/show/id/4353/Job_Cohen_moet_van_de_islam_afblijven, accessed 01 December 2010). She responded to Job Cohen's appeal to draw on the world of academia for our knowledge about Islam and Muslims by listening to the moderate Muslim voice. Ms Kluveld raises the question as to how the moderate voice can be defined.

16   The Pew Research Centre for the People & the Press confirms similar opinions in relation to Muslims living in the United States. A 2007 report states that 'the first-ever, nationwide, random sample survey of Muslim Americans finds them to be largely assimilated, happy with their lives, and moderate with respect to many of the issues that have divided Muslims and Westerners around the world.' (http://people-press. org/report/329/muslim-americans-middle-class-and-mostly-mainstream: accessed 01 December 2010)

17   Fareed Zakaria, *The Future of Freedom: Illiberal Democracy at Home and Abroad* (New York: W.W. Norton & Company; 2003).

A Policymaker's Pressing Questions about Islam

Job Cohen

The increase in interest in the Islam which has transpired in the last decade has everything to do with the events of 9/11, the terrorist attacks of Al-Qaeda on the Twin Towers in New York and the Pentagon in Washington. Since these attacks there have been several more, of which the perpetrators claim to be supporters of the 'true Islam'. The attacks have happened across the whole world: Bali, Istanbul, Casablanca, Hurghada, Madrid, London, Mumbai, etc. and have resulted in many Muslim and non-Muslim fatalities. In the wake of 9/11, the United Nations – supported by troops from all over the world, including the Netherlands – have waged war in Iraq and Afghanistan, leading to estimates of over 100,000 casualties, mostly consisting of civilians.

This led to John Esposito and Dalia Mogahed[1] to write the following in their book *Who speaks for Islam? What a Billion Muslims really think*:

> As we cope with savage actions in a world that seems ever more dangerous and out of control, we are inundated with analyses from terrorism experts and pundits who blame the religion of Islam for global terrorism. At the same time, terrorist groups such as Al-Qaeda beam messages throughout the world that demonize the West as the enemy of Islam and hold it responsible for all the ills of the Muslim world. Amid the rhetoric of hate and growing violence, manifest in both anti-Americanism in the Muslim world and Islamophobia in the West, discrimination against, or hostility toward, Islam or Muslims has massively increased. In the aftermath of 9/11, president George W. Bush emphasized that America was waging a war against terrorism, not against Islam. However, the continued acts by a terrorist minority, statements by preachers of hate (Muslim and Christian alike), anti-Muslim and anti-West talk show hosts, and political commentators have inflamed emotions and distorted views. The religion of Islam and the mainstream Muslim majority have been conflated with the beliefs and actions of an extremist minority.[2]

In the Netherlands, 9/11 is also an important day in this respect. Since then, we have witnessed the rise and murder of the politician Pim Fortuyn in 2002. The filmmaker Theo van Gogh was murdered by an Islamic extremist in 2004. The Dutch, too, face the question of how to deal with these events and the role of Islam in our society.

First, there is the question, 'what can one know and say about Islam in its full diversity: Islam as a religion, as a political factor, as a social, cultural and historical phenomenon, as a poetic source of inspiration, as... you name it. The question is of such size, the perspectives towards the subject are so diverse, the interpretations vary so widely that academic analyses of these questions and perspectives are more than helpful. This brings us to our second question: What can academia tell us about the Islam, about the Muslim world, about the current environment of Muslims in the Netherlands, in Europe, and in all those other countries where Muslims live, whether as a minority or a majority, again in all its diversity? After all, the world of science with its ambition of objectivity and truth, ought to be able to untangle some of the complexities of this debate. Science is indeed able to do so, certainly science as it has been practised at the universities of our country. For, in that respect, Islam and the Muslim world are no new phenomena in Western societies, which we claim to know nothing about. Since many years or even centuries much attention has been paid to the various aspects of Islam and the Muslim world. Yet the knowledge and insights which the world of academia has developed should be better disseminated, and used in domestic politics and policy.

It seems to me that the current public and political discussion about Islam and Muslims in our country ignores this threefold approach. In other words, I believe that all these different interpretations and insights which exist in and in relation to the Muslim world, are not effectively disseminated and therefore play too small a role in the public debate. 'Academia' seems to be overlooked in the public realm. To back up my argument, I would like to refer to the abovementioned book of Esposito and Mogahed.[3] This is a book which is built upon years of research and consultations with thousands of Muslims of different backgrounds in different countries. The book reflects the variety among Muslims, as opposed to focusing on the extremist views which tend to dominate the present discourse. A book, which in spite of positive reviews in the press, was ignored by public opinion and perhaps therefore was hardly able to reach politicians and other policymakers. I should note in this respect that the limited reach of academic knowledge should not only concern journalists and politicians; it is also the academics' responsibility.

So this is one of the most important appeals which I would like to make to academics: please, make sure that evidence-based knowledge and insights do not remain within the academic world, but try your ultimate best to allow these insights to play a role in the public debate. As a former university rector I know that I am digging into an ever-lasting discussion about the tasks of academia. Yet, as the Mayor of Amsterdam, where the debate about Islam has penetrated many discussions, I believe that academics have to make the largest possible effort to place themselves in the middle of this debate. I know that this is not always believed to be one of the core aims of universities, but in my view we are talking about the universities' social responsibility.

When I look at the current debate regarding Islam and Muslims, I notice the following features:

The focus is often on radical, fundamentalist or strictly orthodox variants of Islam, on the fear of terrorism, on the radicalised jihad, on (the preaching for) violence. Without a doubt these are matters – given the past attacks and the fear that they have deliberately caused – against which society wants and needs to arm itself and that is something we see happening. Yet, does this focus give a true representation of Islam and the Muslim world? As an ignoramus, I tend to think: this cannot be so. As is the case in each major religion, Islam too must know many different directions, and a book such as written by Esposito and Mogahed provides an evidence-based argument for this opinion.

In short, I would like to make a public appeal to academia and the media to examine whether the interpretations which shape public opinion about Islam, Muslims and Muslim communities in the Netherlands are supported by an academic body of knowledge. What can the world of academia say about the following ideas which exist in the Netherlands about Islam and Muslim communities?

– Islam is a violent religion;
– The Netherlands is islamising. What does this mean exactly? Is this true? If so, what are the consequences? Is it dangerous? Can it contribute to the development of our society?;
– Is it true that (also internationally) extreme variants of Islam are advancing?;
– Is Islam unchangeable and therefore a 'backward' religion? Is it a religion which is not compatible with contemporary developments of the last few centuries in the West? And is it therefore possible to regard 'the Muslim world', or at least large parts of it, as unchangeable or 'backward'?;
– Does Islam go together with a Western democratic state based on the rule of law? Or broader: is it possible for a Muslim country to be democratic?

Also, there are two further questions which I would like to pose, the first of which is related to Esposito's and Mogahed's book: What do Muslims in the Netherlands want, when it comes down to their participation and integration into Dutch society? What do we know about this? The voice of the 'ordinary' (the common hard-working Muslim, to use the frequent term) Muslim is not heard often in the public debate. There is much to do about radical points of view, and there is much talk about Muslims, but are these accurate reflections of what concerns the average Muslim in our society?

The second question departs from the observation that the Netherlands has a large number of migrants from countries with extensive Muslim communities such as Morocco, Turkey and Surinam; at least that is the case in the large cities. Are there any trends in relation to Islam in these countries of origin which we, in the Netherlands, should keep track of?

I hope that academics as well as the media will engage with these topics and make the dissemination of knowledge and insight for the sake of the public discourse one of their core aims.

Notes

1   See chapter 11 and chapter 12 of this book.
2   John Esposito & Dalia Mogahed, *Who Speaks for Islam? What a billion Muslims really think. Based on Gallup's World Poll – the largest study of its kind* (New York: Gallup Press; 2007).
3   This book appeared in Dutch: John Esposito & Dalia Mogahed, *Wie spreekt namens de Islam?* (Tilburg: Uitgeverij De Wereld; 2008).

Challenges for NATO's Operations in the Muslim World

Jaap de Hoop Scheffer

Towards the end of my term as Secretary General of the NATO I was asked the following question several times during public interviews: 'What have you actually done in five and a half years at NATO in Brussels and in those 28 different countries?'. My answer usually was: 'I felt like the international Job Cohen,[1] I kept the whole thing together.' I meant this in the most positive sense, of course. What I also mean to say is that the type of questions that the former Mayor of Amsterdam, Job Cohen, needed to deal with, had an international dimension. Through globalisation and internationalisation 'the West' is increasingly present in Islamic countries, both politically as well as militarily. In the following, I would like to comment on the dilemmas that this presence leads to, without the pretense of having the solutions.

With regard to our presence in the Muslim world, the term 'normative-neutral' has been used. That raises the question to which extent we are able to be 'normative-neutral'? If we go to Afghanistan – by 'we' meaning the Netherlands, but also the many other countries that are present there – we usually say that we are there in order to protect universal values. One may ask: 'What, then, are these values?'. This is not an easy question to answer. We tend to refer to the universal declaration of human rights. This sounds like the perfect clear-cut answer, but is it the answer to all political questions and does this provide clarity about our role and position, whether political or military, in non-Western countries? The question as to what can be ascribed to religion and what to culture is another interesting one in this respect.

I would briefly like to discuss three cases, examples from my own experience in the last five and half years which touch upon the issue of normative neutrality and the complicated relationship between universal values versus – I pose a question mark after versus – respect for culture and religion in countries where the NATO operates.

You may remember that a few years ago a young man from North-Afghanistan was sentenced to death for downloading a, in our eyes, most innocent text from the internet. There was much consternation about the sentence, and I decided to discuss the issue with the president of Afghanistan, Karzai. I said: 'Mr President, this is an issue that I cannot possibly present at home', to which the president replied: 'what do you mean?'. I answered: 'well, I will clarify what I mean. If there are more than 100,000 troops present in Afghanistan, I need to justify this presence to all the countries involved, the Netherlands, but also Canada, Bulgaria, the United States. I usually tell them that we are here to defend universal values and norms. This sentence that you have just given this young man puts great pressure on this mission.' The president's answer was: 'This may well go against your mission, but it belongs to our culture'. Please note the use of the term 'culture', rather than 'religion'.

Do we witness a clash of values? My second case will make my point clearer. It concerns an Afghan law, which was overlooked by parliament and president, and which – to put it bluntly and without nuance – allowed for rape within marriage. Again, the law caused much public consternation and in my next conversation with president Karzai, I discussed the issue with him in great detail. Finally, his conclusion was, 'being present as a guest in our country with 100,000 troops, you ought to take into consideration our values and legal norms'. I then posed him the question as to how I could explain to the mother or wife of a deceased soldier in Canada or the Netherlands that her son or husband had died in Afghanistan, a country where such norms are put to practice. That leads to the question – an issue which also featured in the discussion of Job Cohen – as to whether we, i.e. the NATO, European Union or United Nations, when present in countries with a different culture or religion, should formulate for ourselves minimum standards of rule of law. Standards that we believe a country should adhere to, and which could justify our presence, our efforts, our money and most importantly, the lives of our soldiers. In all honesty, I admit that I do not have a ready answer, but I do believe that the world of academia in general and LUCIS in particular could play an important role in this debate and add to finding a solution to these problematic questions. On the one hand, one could argue that foreign presence ought to respect a country's history, culture and religion. On the other hand, my examples show that this cannot provide a sufficient answer to the question as to what we can and cannot live with.

I am saying this, because organisations such as the NATO and the European Union, which originate in the Judeo-Christian humanistic culture, are increasingly present in countries and regions with a fundamentally different history, culture and religion and often operate in Islamic countries. The NATO is active in Afghanistan and Kosovo, it trains the Iraqi army, it supports the African Union in Darfur (Sudan) and provided disaster relief in Pakistan after the 2005 earthquake. These activities in Islamic countries bring about many challenges too. For this reason, particularly in the international arena, there is a great need for broadening and expanding our knowledge of Islam. We need to consider what originates in religion or culture and where we draw the line, when trying to answer this question. Once again, I pose the question: 'Are there minimum rule of law standards which we can and ought to expect?' I am making this point set against the background of Afghanistan, a country which after the expulsion of the Taliban regime in 2001 still showed traces of the medieval customs and habits and which is unlikely to be looking like a 'Western' democracy any time soon.

My last case: Jordan. A moderate country in the Middle East ruled by King Abdullah, who plays a most positive role in this debate. When I visited Jordan, I had a most interesting discussion with the king, after which I gave a speech in front of the audience of a Jordanian think-tank. During the Q&A, the audience reproached me by saying that I did not understand them. They asked me what I was doing in Jordan; why the NATO was active in the Middle East; and why I was trying to build relations, as Secretary General of the NATO. I recounted the same stories about Kosovo and Afghanistan, as above. 'There is so much wrong with your image,' they said, and they were not just talking about the NATO, but rather about the whole of the international community, the European Union and all organisations rooted in the same culture. 'There is so much wrong with your image that it will take years to improve that image and win confidence in this region'. My answer was, 'point well taken. Yet, if this is your opinion, may I ask you the same question: how do you think people look upon your reputation on this side [Western] of the world?'

It is my opinion that this latter debate should also be held, within our own countries and internationally. If we wish to continue being active in our foreign policy and if we carry increasing amounts of responsibility in other parts of the world, there is a great need for a better understanding of what we are talking about. During my education at a Roman-Catholic primary and secondary school, there was little mention of Islam or any religion other than Christianity. However, the fact that my daughters, who are now reaching their thirties, did not hear much about non-Western religions, is more surprising. I would therefore like to suggest a change at the school level: if we do not have this discussion and continue to educate another generation in the Netherlands which does not learn about religions outside the Western world, we will continue to see derailments in the debate as we see happening now.

With sufficient knowledge and expertise, it will be easier to enter into discussions with leaders in Islamic countries where we are present, and it will help to prevent the escalation from mutual misunderstanding to unnecessary violence.

Note

1   Jan Jaap de Hoop Scheffer here refers to the position of Job Cohen as the Mayor of Amsterdam (2001-2010). See 'About the Authors'.

The (Ir)Relevance of Academic Research to Foreign Policymaking[1]

Nikolaos van Dam

 **The Kingdom of the Netherlands with the Largest Number of Muslim Citizens in the World**

Who can still remember today that the Kingdom of the Netherlands once upon a time had the largest number of Muslim citizens in the world, because of its colonies in what today is the Republic of Indonesia? And who remembers that the Consulate of the Kingdom of the Netherlands in Jeddah was one of the most important consulates in the world because of the fact that the largest annual contingent of *Hajj* pilgrims was that from the Dutch Indies, who had to pass through the Dutch Consulate on their way to Mecca? With this background it was only logical that Islam was seriously studied by Dutch scholars; and that many of their Islamic studies were related to the situation in the Dutch Indies. Some of the best libraries on the subject were established in the Netherlands and many of the studies that were carried out by Dutch scholars at the time are still valuable today. The libraries and materials are still there, but the number of scholars dealing with Indonesia has drastically declined. So has the interest among students. One would have expected that the Kingdom of the Netherlands of today, formerly being the state with the largest number of Muslim citizens in the world, would be populated by people with special awareness, experience and knowledge about Islam. But this is not the case, and probably never has been so. Two main reasons for this are that the people of Indonesian origin living in the Netherlands are almost exclusively Christians, and that the Dutch in the Indonesian Archipelago generally were not very close with the Muslim communities there, for fear of Islamic opposition and hostility towards Dutch colonialism. This attitude is reflected in the collections of today's Dutch museums. In the Royal Tropical Institute in Amsterdam a lot is exhibited about Indonesian minorities like the Bataks, Dayaks, Papua's, and so on; but hardly anything can be found on the Muslim majority. And this is no coincidence; it was on purpose, because in the past special public attention to the Muslim population was avoided in exhibitions.

The Dutch used to be the academic top elite where Indonesia studies were concerned, but not any longer; although there are still some highly qualified Dutch scholars in this field today.

A Babel-like Confusion of Tongues and the Fixation on Islam

Today's interest in Islam, and the discussions about it, have obtained completely different dimensions. It seems there is sometimes a Babel-like confusion of tongues. Many people talk about Islam these days as if it were a fixation. And when people discuss Islam, they sometimes have completely different things in mind. Some talk about various regions in the world, each having different cultures, from Morocco to Indonesia, and wrongly imagine that they are talking about the same subject; some talk about Muslim immigrants in Europe, but ignore the fact that these people are not always representative of the societies in their countries of origin; some talk about terrorism, and identify Islam with violence; some about sharia being applied in different forms, some about the Taliban in Afghanistan, some about the Ahmadiyah, and so on. Many of these discussions are often closely linked to our daily lives or to our foreign policies, instead of really having to do with Islam as a religion. As a result, there is a lot of room for confusion, particularly if people talk about completely different things without even being aware of it.

Serving in the Islamic World

Almost 35 years ago, I started working at the Ministry of Foreign Affairs in The Hague. During this period I had the luck of always being posted in places that had my highest interest. Most of the time I lived in Arab or Islamic countries – mainly at my personal request. First in Lebanon and Libya; and later as ambassador to Iraq, Egypt and Turkey; and now in Indonesia. Only once did I serve as ambassador to a non-Islamic country, notably Germany, although I should add that in Ankara Berlin is labelled as being the largest Turkish city outside Turkey.

Before joining the Ministry I was active in the academic field. Having studied Arabic and Political & Social Sciences, I did field studies in Syria, Iraq and Lebanon, and obtained my PhD on modern Syrian political history. Originally, I had foreseen an academic career, but more or less by coincidence I joined the Foreign Ministry. Nevertheless, until the present day, I have always remained loyal to my academic interests, and combined them with my work, whenever this was possible. As a result, I have been in a position to closely observe the issue of 'the relevance (or perhaps irrelevance) of academic research to foreign policymaking'.

I can do so as an insider on both sides, and therefore feel sufficiently equipped to make some remarks based on practical experience.

Generalists and Specialists

When I started at the Ministry of Foreign Affairs in The Hague the prevalent approach was that of *generalism*. Diplomats were supposed to be able to be posted anywhere in the world, and therefore should be generalists. Specialists, on the other hand, were supposed to be less suitable to carry out general tasks all over the world, and should for this simple reason be guided and directed by generalists. My first director at the Ministry of Foreign Affairs argued that I was a specialist who only knew something about the Middle East, and by implication was therefore less qualified to do any other tasks. Even when I told him that I had also graduated *cum laude* in Political & Social Sciences, which can be considered as one of the most generalist studies, he was not convinced. A specialist remains a specialist, and is therefore less capable of doing work which falls outside the scope of his specialism. In other words, by obtaining more specialist knowledge, one is supposed to be capable of doing less. Fortunately, such irrational ways of reasoning have become less common, be it that in practice the value of specialism is still strongly underrated.

The Ministry of Foreign Affairs is obliged to rotate its diplomats more or less every four years, and therefore does not always have the 'luxury' to keep rotating specialists only within their region of specialisation, apparently because there are not enough of them. That is one of the reasons why the Ministry keeps trying to recruit more Arabists, Sinologists and other linguists in an effort to help solve this problem. But it is apparently more difficult than it appears at first sight. When I started 35 years ago, a pilot project was started to attract more Arabists. But the results have been far from impressive, if not very disappointing. In the eighteen Dutch diplomatic representations which today cover the Arab world there is presently not one single Foreign Ministry diplomat who is an Arabist. A new pilot project has been started, and two Arabist trainees have been recruited, but the problem will remain as long as specialists are not kept for longer periods in their areas of specialisation.

The Practical Use of Specialist Knowledge

It is obvious that a specialist, who is posted in the country of his specialisation, can achieve much more than a non-specialist, at least if he can combine his expertise with other qualifications needed for his job, be it as an ambassador, as staff member of an embassy section in the field of economics, development cooperation, political affairs, press and cultural affairs, and so on. But his personality and communicative capabilities also count strongly. If he does not possess the right skills in this respect, a capable non-specialist might achieve even more. Many non-specialist diplomats can obtain extensive knowledge within the period of their posting, but the possibilities are of course limited by the duration of their stay, which on average is only four years.

Just being a linguist is not enough, however. Excellent knowledge of, for instance, the Arabic language, does in no way guarantee that an Arabist is better qualified to be an expert on the Arab world or specific Arab countries than a non-Arabist. To achieve this, a lot of additional work and studies are required. On the other hand, it goes without saying that an Arabist has many more possibilities to go into depth when wanting to study the Arab world, or certain aspects of it. But he must also really do it, instead of just having the potential of doing so. As a specialist in the Islamic and Arab world I have always enjoyed an enormous advantage over non-specialist colleagues. Being fluent in the local language, both in its official form and in dialects, combined with being well versed in the local culture and history, is a decisive key to success. I am convinced that the Ministry of Foreign Affairs and its embassies abroad could do their jobs very well if the necessary expertise would not only be available somewhere in the Ministry apparatus, but would be adequately used in the right place.

Is Outside Academic Expertise Really Needed?

Does this mean that in case there is no specialist knowledge available on a specific topic that we have to get our expertise from elsewhere? From outside the Ministry in the academic world? From academic specialists, including linguists? Or can the Ministry manage to solve such a problem by itself? The answer very much depends on what type of problems or questions are to be solved, and how operational or crucial the role of the Netherlands really is. Quite another aspect is that the presence of expertise in itself is not enough. There should also be a willingness on the side of the government to seriously listen to expert views. It sounds obvious, but in practice such willingness is not always there.

Snouck Hurgronje's Advice (ambtelijke adviezen) on Aceh

Just take the role of Islamic society in certain countries: What do we need to know about it in order to cover our bilateral relations properly? The need for specialist knowledge is much more urgent when a country is a real key player than when it is just an observer. When the Netherlands was still a colonial power in the Indonesian Archipelago, it was highly relevant to have such specialist knowledge. By way of an example, the well-known Dutch Arabist and Islam expert Snouck Hurgronje, who was advisor to the Dutch colonial government, at the time played an essential role because of his detailed studies on the people of Aceh. By providing detailed studies about Acehnese society, he could make a crucial contribution by explaining which (Machiavellian) tactics and strategies could best be followed in order to defeat and subdue the Acehnese. The bloody war in Aceh therewith came to an end after more than 30 years.

Preventing Stoning (rajam) in Aceh

Today the situation for the Netherlands is completely different. We are fortunately not a colonial power anymore. Nevertheless we want to be informed well enough so as to be able to adequately carry out our operational policies. Take for instance the newly introduced draft bylaw in Aceh on stoning people to death (*rajam*). We are against such a development and want to counter it if possible. But what to do about it? Of course we need to be well informed first, but we do not need an academic study of several months or years about the state of affairs concerning sharia regulations in Indonesia in order to help prevent these regulations from being effectuated. Usually we do not have the luxury of being able to wait such a long time before taking practical action. For that aim we need good contacts and exchanges of views with the Indonesian parties directly concerned. And in order to achieve appropriate results, we need to have the right contacts and the right persons to carry out the task of directly convincing people. With some effort we can obtain enough essential expertise from within Indonesia.

Fitnah

Something similar was the case when in 2008 protests erupted in Indonesia because of the badly received film 'Fitnah' of Dutch parliamentarian Geert Wilders, who identifies Islam with violence and terrorism. The most important thing for me to counter the protests and demonstrations was by communicating face-to-face with a high diversity of Islamic groups, both moderate (such as the Muhammadiyah and the Nahdat al-Ulema) and more radical (such as Hizbut Tahrir), and by having an open dialogue with them in Indonesian (and occasionally also in Arabic), both behind closed doors, as well as in front of the media. Fortunately, I already had a wide network of contacts with various Islamic parties long before these problems started, as a result of which many difficulties could be overcome relatively easily. I could, however, never have delegated my task – which also had a strong public relations component – to an outside academic expert. I needed to have the knowledge and expertise myself.

 Military Intervention in Iraq, Afghanistan or Lebanon

Let me give some other practical examples about the relevance (or irrelevance) of academic research to foreign policymakers. What to do if the Netherlands wants to cooperate in military operations in, for instance, Lebanon, Iraq or Afghanistan? Do our ministers consult academic experts from outside the government administration before coming to a decision? Most probably not. Generally, they will want to consult with experts from within their own ministries, including law experts. This is yet another reason why it is so important to have our own experts within the ministries. But in the end it remains a political choice and decision, to be made by the government and its ministers.

What did the United States do before attacking Iraq in 2003? Academic advice may have been sought in the US, and certainly also the advice of some intelligence services. But in the end primarily political motives prevailed. Academic advice which was not supportive of the chosen policy line generally would be ignored, if not criticised with insinuations of disloyalty and disturbing unity among allies. It was only after the US occupation of Iraq that some US academic experts were recruited to help find out how the US presence could best be brought to a satisfactory end. Also outside the United States, criticism of the foreign intervention in Iraq in 2003 (and afterwards) was generally not welcomed, at least by the governments of those countries which had supported the US intervention.

In many other countries all over the world, it would not be very different, when it really comes to highly political and controversial issues. The advice of experts would not really always be appreciated if it would be contrary to what the ministers or their governments had in mind. A ministry official might put forward a deviant or contrary advice once or perhaps twice, or even three times, but then it would be better for him/her to stop. After all, it is the government and its ministers who decide, and they have the prerogative to determine the political course to be taken. And ministers have to take the internal and external political factors into account. Their own governmental positions might even be at stake.

Israel and Palestine: Does Knowledge Change Political Positions?

To give yet another example: Take the policies of Western countries towards Israel. They have not changed very much over the years, even though much more is known and acknowledged now about the numerous Israeli violations of international law, of human rights or war crimes in the Palestinian occupied territories. More knowledge and more academic research have, however, not led to important changes in the daily policies of European governments. The well-researched book recently published by former prime minister and prominent CDA party member Mr Dries Van Agt, titled *Een schreeuw om recht. De tragedie van het Palestijnse volk*, [A Cry for Justice. The Tragedy of the Palestinian People] has been taken note of by the Ministry of Foreign Affairs, but Van Agt's book will most probably not change anything, irrespective of his four years of painstaking work. I guess it will rather be considered as a nuisance and that it will further be ignored. Van Agt's work is a clear case of unsolicited academic advice which is not really welcomed.

Papua

Yet another example, but within a completely different context, is the academic study of Dr P.J. Drooglever, *Een daad van vrije keuze* [An Act of Free Choice] about the decolonisation of Indonesia and the right to self-determination of the Papua's. The research was commissioned by the Minister of Foreign Affairs, at the explicit request of the Dutch Parliament. But by the time Drooglever's study was completed, the Dutch Government, in its contacts with both the Indonesian Government, as well as with the Dutch Parliament, had to stress time and again that this research was a purely academic affair, which in no way affected the policies of the Dutch Government, which stress the support for Indonesia's territorial integrity and unity. Drooglever's study had to be ignored because it would otherwise probably have been misused for political purposes.

Studies for the Embassy in Jakarta

At the request of the Netherlands Ministry of Foreign Affairs a research project was carried out for the Embassy in Jakarta under supervision of Professor Martin van Bruinessen, involving four Indonesian scholars. The result was a 225-page long study titled: *Contemporary Developments in Indonesian Islam. Explaining the 'Conservative Turn'*. One of the main questions is what the practical use of this study has been for the embassy. I conclude that, however interesting the report may be – and it is indeed interesting and instructive – its impact for practical use has been limited. We already have dozens of studies available on Islam in Indonesia (including some highly interesting studies by Van Bruinessen himself), and the subject is also being dealt with in the Indonesian media on a daily basis. Therefore, I do not really need to commission additional studies for my personal use, except of course if there would be a very specific need, for which we cannot find any alternative material. But let us first read the most important works that already exist; preferably with the advice of some scholars about which works we should give priority to. As for the embassy staff, I think it is much more rewarding for them to explore Islamic issues themselves in direct encounters with Indonesians in several Indonesian provinces, so as to get their first-hand impressions themselves and to build up their own network of contacts and obtain personal expertise, which then later can be used for practical embassy purposes.

If future studies were to be carried out, its practical purposes should be taken into account to the maximum; and a higher frequency of contacts between the embassy – both the ambassador and his staff – and the researchers should be encouraged, to be able to get the necessary feedback which might provide chances to adapt our course, whenever needed. And to learn something in the meantime by discussing the issues at hand. But also without such specific studies being carried out, regular contacts between diplomats and scholars should be encouraged, to create a better symbiosis between policymakers and scholars.

Expertise Should Be Highly Valued and Cherished

This being said, I nevertheless strongly support academic studies such as those carried out under the supervision of Professor van Bruinessen. After all, the development of Dutch academic expertise in this field should be encouraged. Expertise on Indonesia has already dramatically declined over the last decades, irrespective of the fact that the Republic of Indonesia remains one of our most important partners in Asia, as is also reflected by the fact that our embassy in Jakarta is the largest Dutch embassy in the world. But whether such studies are really relevant to foreign policymaking is a different matter. Bilateral relations are, however, more than foreign policy alone. They also include scientific cooperation and many other fields.

I would like to stress that I think it is also essential for the Ministry of Foreign Affairs and other ministries, to further build up and develop the necessary expertise amongst their own staff, *and* to make the maximum use of it. Expertise should be highly valued and cherished.

Making Academic Research and Expertise More Relevant

Let me conclude by saying that it is no secret that in the past, some political decision makers of various countries have made historical mistakes with disastrous consequences, partially as a result of the fact that they ignored the good advice of their specialist staff or of academic experts; or by not having sufficient internal expertise and knowledge within their own administrations. When evaluating the course of events in the past, I do not have the illusion that something similar will not happen again in the future. Let me nevertheless end by expressing the optimistic wish that experts and scholars will persevere in their efforts to put their academic research and experience at the disposal of foreign policymakers in such a way that it will make their work really relevant.

Note

1   These personal remarks were given on the occasion of the conference 'Studying Islam in the Public Sphere: A Critical Reflection on Knowledge Production' (Leiden, 3 November 2009).

Dynamism in Islamic Activism: Some Reflections on the Advisory Report by the WRR (Netherlands Scientific Council for Government Policy)

Wendy Asbeek Brusse

I was asked to reflect briefly on the realisation, the reception, the political reaction to and the ramifications of a report published by the WRR (Netherlands Scientific Council for Government Policy) entitled *Dynamism in Islamic Activism*, which appeared in April 2006.[1] I was also asked to comment briefly on the relationship between academia and policy by means of a number of propositions on the polarised issue of Islam.

Please allow me to start with the background to the WRR's research project. Towards the end of 2002, Islamic activism as an issue was placed on the agenda of the WRR. In the following years, the issue of 'Islam' also became increasingly controversial among EU countries and in the Netherlands. During the Dutch presidency of the EU in 2004, the European Council was faced with the question whether to start negotiations with Turkey on accession to the European Union. Ordinary citizens as well as several Dutch parliamentarians seemed to feel uncomfortable with Turkey on the grounds of it being a *Muslim* country. They were wondering whether a country with a majority Muslim population would fit in with the democratic values of the EU. Therefore, the WRR first tried to address this matter.

In its report entitled *The European Union, Turkey and the Islam* the WRR stated that Turkish Islam in principle would not form an obstacle to full participation within the EU. This recommendation was based on the following findings:
- The historically strong roots of the Turkish secular state (as was also demonstrated by Leiden University's professor Erik-Jan Zürcher in a study commissioned by the WRR);
- Within the current member states of the EU, there is a wide variety in formal and actual relations between church and state. There is no such thing as one single yardstick with which to confront Turkey;
- The gradual modernisation and democratisation of political landscape, society and religion in Turkey;

– This being said, Turkey still has a long way to go before meeting all
  formal membership requirements (the so-called Copenhagen
  Criteria, including the full freedom of religion).

The timing of this advice, which appeared just before the start of the
Dutch presidency of the EU, was well chosen. This timing certainly
served the Dutch prime minister at the time, Jan Peter Balkenende,
who in his address to the European Parliament on 21 July, 2004, stated
'Islam is not the problem'.

In the formal reaction to the WRR's report that appeared several
months later, the Dutch cabinet responded as follows: 'The analysis of
the WRR provides us with convincing evidence that Islam, as adhered
to by the Turkish population, is hugely diverse. The majority in Turkey
supports a moderate version of Islam. There is no evidence that this
will change as the country is easing the current restrictions to democracy and the freedom of religion.'

Two years after this, the WRR report *Dynamism in Islamic Activism*
appeared. By this time, the political climate in the Netherlands had
become polarised further. This report thus started from the evident
assumption that since 9/11, the war in Iraq and the murder of Theo
van Gogh, Islam and Muslims had widely become associated with
purely negative manifestations such as terrorism and intolerance
towards democracy and human rights. Therefore, the WRR decided to
look into potentially *constructive* elements within Islamic activism,
which could provide starting points for democratisation and human
rights' improvements.

The WRR's report examined three dimensions: the developments in political thinking, in political and social movements and in law. It concen-
trated mainly on global, international and foreign developments, but
also paid some attention to manifestations of Islam within the
Netherlands itself.

The research findings resulting from these examinations can be sum-
marised by the terms 'dynamism' and 'diversity'. According to the
report, there is no academic evidence for the idea that Islam is general
and 'the' Muslim world would be diametrically opposed to 'our' democratic values and human rights. There are many modern thinkers, who
– often also on Islamic grounds – argue for the separation of mosque
and state and who dedicate themselves to improvements in democracy
and human rights. Moreover, there are Islam-oriented, political movements which – although previously working against the state – now
wish to play a more constructive role within their own nation states. As
a result, a wide range of opinions has developed between and within
Muslim countries about the relation between Islam and politics,

democracy and human rights. The general public in the Netherlands, however, seems to be unaware of this diversity.

Ultimately, the WRR has to be relevant to *government policy*. Its core recommendations for policy were essentially the following:

1 There are some elements within Islamic activism for improving democracy and human rights, but they are fragile, especially set against the background of political unrest in Iraq, the Middle East, Afghanistan and the international war against terrorism. At the same time, the EU and the Netherlands cannot continue to isolate themselves from their neighbouring Muslim countries. There is need for constructive engagement.
2 There is need for differentiation and pragmatism. The Dutch government should recognise that Islamic movements have the potential to contribute towards democratic development in the Muslim world. It should judge Muslims on account of their actions, and not merely on their (religious) words. It should engage with endogenous development strategies.
3 This requires more specific knowledge about the various local, political, societal, legal and intellectual developments, both on a national and international level. It is important to invest in building and extending that knowledge.
4 Out of national interest, it is important to invest in informed public opinion and debate about Islam and Muslims.

Dynamism in Islamic Activism appeared in a strongly polarised climate. The responses from the media and the public ranged from extremely positive to extremely negative. The main point of criticism was that the WRR appeared to be naïve, apologetic and unscientific. The following citation from the parliamentary debate illustrates this point: 'The National Counter Terrorism Centre has made a list of religious attacks committed worldwide. The total is 1563, four of which were carried out by Jews, 48 by Christians, and 1511 by Muslims. If the WRR does not mention these facts, it passes over the sentiment of the population. Orthodox religion and radicalisation are increasing. These issues are understated in the report.'

This, in a nutshell, also illustrates the difference between the role chosen by the WRR and the role of an experienced politician in a media-driven democracy. The WRR sought for nuance and windows of opportunity for government policy on the basis of factual academic analyses. The politician named the popular sentiment and 'reframed' the problem accordingly. His policy recommendation included: never enter into discussions with radical Islamic movements.

The official reaction of the cabinet on the report of the WRR contained more nuance (chapter six in this volume). I will cite just one key passage:

> The WRR believes it is necessary to base its policy perspectives on the knowledge of the actual developments within and characteristics of Islamic activism. Yet, the WRR still decided to focus its research on the positive sides (...) and pay no attention to the 'widely known negative manifestations.' One of the consequences is that according to the cabinet's point of view (...) the report presents a more rosy picture of Islamic activism than would be the case if all aspects of Islamic activism had been considered. This limited perspective, however, is justified in view of the research question that the WRR posed. When the question is whether black swans exist, one merely needs to find one without the need of counting all the white swans.

I will be brief about the practical ramifications of the report. It is my impression that, as yet, the report is only known to a small circle of cabinet, parliament, directly involved policymakers, Islam experts and the intellectual spheres in the Dutch Muslim communities. The WRR made a concerted effort to present the report to a wider public. This coincided with a brief but intense debate. However, its message did not reach, let alone convince, a broader public. Perhaps this is also too much to ask in the current, highly polarised political climate. Moreover, experience tells us that policy advice by the WRR often needs more than just one or two years of incubation time to work its way into the 'mainstream' through circles of professionals, academics and NGOs. The recent uprisings in the Arab world and the windows of opportunities this offers for political and legal reforms, may well revive interest in the WRR's analysis and policy recommendations.

This leads me to the following propositions:
1   There is a continued need for academically-founded information about Islam within the public debate, policy and politics.
2   Academics should also contribute to 'de-religionising' the debate about migrants.
3   The times that academic research could count on natural authority in society are over once and for all. To gain influence, academics and policymakers should be aware of 'the logic' of media and politics. They need a keen eye for the timing of their message, they need to repeat it frequently to different audiences and be available to answer knowledge questions from the press, stakeholders, politicians and the wider public in an open and honest manner.

Note

1   Wetenschappelijke Raad for het Regeringsbeleid, *Dynamiek in islamitisch activisme: aanknopingspunten voor democratisering and mensenrechten* (Amsterdam: Amsterdam University Press; 2006). Also published in English: WRR (Scientific Council for Government Policy), *Dynamism in Islamic Activism. Reference Points for Democratization and Human Rights* (Amsterdam: Amsterdam University Press; 2006).

Excerpts from the Cabinet's Reaction[1] to the WRR report *Dynamism in Islamic Activism: Reference Points for Democratization and Human Rights*[2]

Since 1972, the WRR (Scientific Council for Government Policy), a prominent Dutch public think tank, has played an important role in the dynamic interplay between policy, academic research, public opinion and politics in the Netherlands. The Dutch government is legally obliged to respond officially and formulate its own opinions on matters raised by WRR reports. From 2003-2006, the WRR conducted a major study on whether Islamic activism could offer reference points for democracy and human rights. Their report, published in April 2006, did indeed note a number of important positive reference points, and understandably the report and its underlying studies were hotly debated in the media. Only in July 2007, was the official cabinet response published, after an unusually long period of political and interdepartmental deliberations, and a change of government.[3] As the official response is in fact the only document representing the view of any Dutch cabinet on Islam and its role in the government's policy, the editors have chosen to include some excerpts of an edited translation.

On Islam, Diversity and Human Rights

'The WRR believes that the diversity within Islamic activism provides reference points for policies which strengthen human rights and democratisation in the Muslim world, for the diversity shows that the assumption that the Islam is fundamentally in conflict with those values is incorrect.' (p. 7)

On the Diversity of Religious and Ideological Interpretations

'In respect of the relationship between Islam and the democratic rule of law, one can refer to the analyses which circulate in the Islamic world based on Islamic sources, as well as the more profound values which Islam, Christianity and Judaism have in common and which partly build the foundation for the principles of humanity and universal human rights. Here one needs to recognise that – religious and political (eds.) – ideologies as such do not determine the way in which a society is shaped, but that this depends more on the presence or absence of tolerance or appreciation of diversity. History shows that both religious as well as non-religious convictions can be interpreted in such a way that it can lead to dictatorial regimes, fake democracies and oppression, but also in ways that lead to democratic rule of law, providing optimal freedom to its citizens.' (p. 21-22)

On Democratisation and Human Rights as Essential Conditions

'The WRR rightly calls democratisation and the strengthening of human rights central themes of both Dutch and European foreign policy. It concerns not goals in their own right, but concrete conditions for the more general aim of ensuring and strengthening a peaceful and rights-based international society, in which peoples and persons are respected and are able to develop. Advancement and protection of human rights and democracy do not depend on altruistic idealism, but on the recognition that these are essential conditions for sustainable cohabitation of people and peoples and the coexistence of countries in peace, justice and prosperity.' (p. 7)

[...]

'Promoting human rights and democracy as central aims of foreign policy therefore does not stem from a missionary zeal to impose specific political values, but rather from the aim to build a strong foundation for a national and international political (legal) order that offers people the opportunity to free themselves from fear and deprivation, regardless of sex, ethnicity, religion or social status, and thus establish the necessary conditions for peace and justice in the world. This is not about Western values versus other cultures and beliefs, but rather about the advancement of an open, inclusive political system versus local, national, political and social orders which exist next to and exclude each other.' (p. 8)

On Universality of Human Rights and Neutrality of Religion

'Concerning the universality of human rights and the necessity of democratic systems and good governance, it is concluded that "the West" in promoting these matters cannot appropriate the definition of democracy and human rights; however, it can support processes which can lead to their strengthening. With regards to neutrality towards religion, it is emphasised that [...] the government always approaches people as citizens, not as adherents of a particular ideology – religious or political (eds).' (p. 4)

On Religion: Cohesive or Dividing?

'Fundamental to the choices that the cabinet makes, is the conviction that religion and social action based on religious conviction can contribute positively to the cohesion of society. At the same time it is evident that a strong emphasis on religious identity can also cause a chasm and that this risk increases when religious dividing lines coincide with other divisions, such as social, cultural and economic divisions. It is also clear that religious activism which is in conflict with the principles of democracy and the rule of law, or which aims for goals which violate universal human rights, has to be rejected – and where it poses a serious threat, should be fought.' (p. 3)

On Secularism and Room for Religion

'The separation between church and state does [...] not mean that religion and the democratic state are not (allowed to be) connected at all. Convictions – or philosophies of life – provide the foundation for all human action and therefore also for the relations between people and the way in which they organise society. Religions do not differ from other convictions in this respect. As a consequence, religions present in a particular society can influence the functioning of the state and the state, whilst structuring society, can influence and sometimes, if need be, engage with the way in which religions are practised and expressed. In that sense, issues such as religiously-inspired political parties and tax-funded religiously-inspired schools, but also the legal effect under private law of church weddings – which is not accepted in the Netherlands –, are in principle not in conflict with the idea of separation of church and state. The separation is only affected if religious authorities through their position (try to) exercise governmental or political power, or if the state apparatus intervenes substantially in religions or religious convictions of individuals or in the internal functioning of religious communities and their institutions.' (p. 12)

On Rejection of Legal pluralism within the Dutch Legal System

'With regards to [...] legal pluralism the cabinet takes the position that the law in the Netherlands should be in agreement with universal human rights and that it applies equally to all. This last point means that it is not possible to have different legal systems which exist alongside each other. Whoever wishes to aim for this needs to realise that the Dutch legal system provides ample freedom to arrange one's own life as he/she wishes, as long as it is not in conflict with the values of democracy and the rule of law.' (p. 5)

'The cabinet [in the Netherlands] cannot support legal pluralism, meaning the equal co-existence of heterogeneous legal systems. This is evident in the case of administrative and criminal law, as these deal with the relation between state and citizen, and the state does not discriminate between types of citizens. In the case of civil law, and in particular the law of obligation, personal status and family law, there is no reason for such legal pluralism. The Dutch state maintains the principle that everyone who resides in the Netherlands should have as much opportunity as possible to organise his/her own life in the way he/she wishes. [...] The cabinet, therefore, aims to offer spaces in its law and policy for traditions which, though they do not belong to the national heritage, are in themselves not in conflict with basic principles.' (p.27)

On Foreign Policy's Need for Knowledge

'Because of the fact that in the process of realising the goals of foreign policy with regards to democracy and human rights there is need for a level of restraint – if not only for the principle of non-intervention in domestic affairs of other states – cooperation with local partners is very important. Effective policy is based on broad knowledge and therefore also about partners for dialogue, which is not immediately self-evident. We need partners for dialogue with whom we agree about principal notions, such as democracy and human rights. This does not mean that beforehand we must share the same opinion on how these goals should be achieved. It is for this reason important to conduct a clear dialogue in a respectful manner, a dialogue in which problems are not hidden. Possessing knowledge about the local community and the right social networks to make this possible belongs to the duties of the representatives of the Netherlands in the relevant countries. It is hereby important to have insight into the role of religion, both from a purely political as a developmental perspective. Cooperation with private development organisations and other NGOs can be important, because they have access to different types of networks. [...]' (p. 13)

On Freedom of Expression and Role of the State

'The WRR referred explicitly to the sense of distrust which has arisen around "the Islam" and the sometimes negative tone of debates about the Islam or debates in which Islam is considered the cause of problems within society. These are indeed matters of concern, but the state can only bear a limited responsibility in countering these developments.

For the freedom of expression leaves room for expressions, which many or at least the people who are closely involved, regard as shocking or badly informed – as long as they remain within the framework of the law and legal practices and are therefore not regarded as insulting or discriminating, or inciting hatred, according to judicial criteria. The cabinet, however, still wishes to emphasise the importance of a well-informed debate that is conducted with mutual respect. Points of view based on knowledge are more beneficial than opinions based merely on a lack of familiarity or fear. And whilst expressions which – whether intentionally or not – are offensive, may be more capable of reaching another person than careful wording, they are not necessarily more effective in transferring the message. Partly for this reason, it is important that the government (local and national) reacts to radical expressions, regardless of their nature. [...]' (p. 18)

Notes

1   'Kabinetsreactie rapport 73: Dynamiek in islamitisch activisme', http://www.wrr.nl/content.jsp?objectid=4066 (accessed 10 August 2011)
2   Wetenschappelijke Raad voor het Regeringsbeleid *Dynamiek in islamitisch activisme: aanknopingspunten voor democratisering and mensenrechten* (Amsterdam: Amsterdam University Press; 2006). Also published in English: WRR (Scientific Council for Government Policy), *Dynamism in Islamic Activism. Reference Points for Democratization andHuman Rights* (Amsterdam: Amsterdam University Press; 2006).
3   The WRR presented the report to the Dutch cabinet in April 2006. In July 2006 the second cabinet under prime minister Jan Peter Balkenende fell, and was replaced by a third cabinet under PM Balkenende (July 2006-February 2007). However, the official response to the report was not made public until the fourth cabinet under PM Balkenende, which came to power in February 2007.

Historical Diversity in the Muslim World

Petra Sijpesteijn

The focus of my research is on the history of Islam, especially the first two centuries of its existence – that is, from the time of the Prophet Muhammad at the beginning of the seventh century until the ninth century, when the Islamic civilisation was at its medieval peak.

Within a hundred years of the death of Muhammad in 632, spectacular conquests had brought the Arabs control of an area stretching from Spain to China. The speed and extent of these conquests still amaze. Any assessment of the rise of Islam, therefore, is dominated by an over-riding question: How was this possible? How could a movement that had arisen among tribesmen on the Arabian peninsula, at the outer margins of the then civilised world, have so quickly become the rulers of an empire of this scale?

This question leads almost immediately to another one: How did the Muslims manage to hold these domains? The Middle East has had no shortage of conquerors, but they came and (eventually) went. With very few exceptions, the Muslims are still there. What did the Muslims bring with them in terms of cultural, political, military and religious experience and organisation that made them so successful? The instinct for governing seems to have been there from the beginning, but where did it come from? What *was* Islam at this time and how does it relate to the Islam of modern-day Muslims?

These questions are rendered especially problematic because we have no contemporary Arabic books from this crucial period. All relevant historical, legal and religious texts date from the ninth century, two centuries after the events they describe and from a time when ideas about what Islam should be and how it had come about were fully formed. This does not mean that the later sources are useless, but we cannot solely rely on them to understand early Islam.

We need, in short, other – independent and contemporary – sources. And this is what I work on: the use of archaeological material, coins, inscriptions and documents written on papyrus from the first two centuries of Islam. These documentary sources were never intended to be read by later generations. Their uses were fixed in precise and limited moments, and when those moments had passed, they were discarded.

The subject matter of these documents is by nature mundane and often seemingly trivial, but its very everydayness also makes it uniquely fresh, offering us a direct window into the lives and daily concerns of the period.

I use these documents in combination with the later literary sources to look at the impact of the Arab invaders in the territories they conquered. How do we encounter the conquerors, as soldiers, government officials and tax collectors, traders, husbands and wives? How were they recognisable as newcomers, through their language, names, cultural or religious practices? And what changed under their rule? With this evidence I study two concurrent processes: the geographical spread of Islam as a movement; and the formation of Islam as a (remarkably resilient) system of ideas. To counter the Islamic exceptionalism that has often marked the field, I view the processes of conquest, acculturation, multilingualism, conversion and administrative reform that resulted from the arrival of the Arabs in the context of similar events and changes that have taken place in the Middle East and beyond. Some aspects of these processes were unique to the Muslim conquests; others, on the other hand, compare well with similar events of political change in the region.

It is clear that Islam in these first two centuries was something quite different from the Islam we know today. At the same time, many of Islam's key precepts and elements were already present in the early period. The challenge is to chart – and explain – Islam's evolution without lapsing into easy explanations of essentialism on the one hand and opportunism on the other.

There is No 'Pure' Early Islam

Islam did not enter the world complete and fully formed with the revelations of Muhammad: key issues remained to be resolved by his successors. Most strikingly, given Muhammad's political astuteness, he left behind no blueprint for the movement's organisation beyond his death, no roadmap or 'strategic plan' to address the question of 'where to go from here?' Most glaringly, when he did die in 632 A.D., the critical question of his succession was entirely open. Not only was Islam without an anointed successor, there was not even a leadership model. Who was to lead the Muslim community on its ongoing path to salvation? And along which path? Solutions were, by necessity, improvised, and became, not surprisingly, matters of urgent debate, in which a variety of subgroups – Muslim elders, later converts, Muhammad's wives and faithful friends – jostled to assert their views. Different ideas, partially based on kingship models current in the region, fought for acceptance: Should Muhammad's successor be related to him by blood, family or tribe? Was he supposed to be an early convert or was his social position in Arabian society to take precedence? Did the successor have to be male or could it also be a woman? Freeborn or slave? Arab or non-Arab? Elected or appointed? For the more intractable differences of opinion, given what was at stake, the inevitable result was war. The uncertainty was first expressed by the Arab tribes that had been united under Muhammad's rule and considered their obedience to have been to the Prophet personally and to his religion. They did not see any necessity in transferring their allegiance to his successor and withdrew to their own territories. Abu Bakr (r. 632-634), the first caliph, managed through a series of battles, which became known as the *ridda* wars, the wars of apostasy, to bring these seceding tribes back into the *umma*, the community of believers. The discussion continued under the three subsequent successors of Muhammad, cumulating in the first *fitnah* (civil war) lasting from 656 to 661. The fourth caliph, 'Ali, Muhammad's cousin and son-in-law, had been a favourite for the caliphate after the death of the Prophet, especially amongst those in the community who considered family ties to be the cornerstone of succession. Others, however, were prepared to fight 'Ali over his right to assume the mantle of leadership. The legacy of these conflicts still defines the major schisms in Islam, with the followers of Muhammad's favourite wife and one of the most important authorities for his life, 'A'isha, coalescing into the Sunnis, and the followers of 'Ali, becoming the Shi'ites. A third group, the Khārijites, still surviving as the Ibāḍī of Oman, Zanzibar and North Africa, split from 'Ali's camp (and later in 661 killed him), when he attempted to broker a compromise with his challengers.

This first *fitnah* remains heavy with symbolism and meaning for Muslims because it so violently belied the ideal of Muslim unity. Paradoxically, the period following Muhammad's death, when the Muslim capital was still based in Medina on the Arabian peninsula, which is traditionally looked upon as Islam's purest and brightest age, is also one of its most turbulent and divisive. The instability of the early period is exemplified by the assassination of three of the four original 'rightly guided' caliphs, albeit not all for political-religious reasons, and by its many revolts and religious splinter groups settling on the fringes of the Islamic Empire.

The question of leadership was such a contentious one because religion and politics were so closely linked. The rightly guided *imam*, or pastor, defined the community of believers – without him there could be no *umma*[1] and no salvation.[2] So important was this function that a political leader deemed inadequate to the task could face removal; indeed, for some Muslims, such a perception provided a legitimate warrant for usurpation. Conversely, political conflicts immediately acquired religious overtones, with bad leaders branded *ipso facto* bad Muslims. This is an ongoing debate. Questions about what constitutes a right, religious leader, and what to do if such a leader is not available, and what happens to Muslims who find themselves under non-Muslim leadership – can they still be saved? – remain fundamental to Muslim political discourse to this day.

It is the *format* of this debate that is authentic, not any specific solution. Attempts to posit a 'pure' Islam, therefore, at the time of the Prophet and directly afterwards misrepresent this process: the Islam to which Muslim puritans would return is only one variant of Muslim social and political organisation. It gives primacy to a model that (to the extent we can reconstruct it) was unlikely to have been considered, even by its own adherents, definitive and absolute; rather it was only one of the many expressions of an ongoing conversation. It is important to emphasise this point – whether one is motivated by idealism or essentialism – one misinterprets Muslim history by neglecting the constant debate and struggle for definition.

 Islam and Muslim Communities Have Never Been Monolithic

Throughout the entire history of Islam there has been debate and discussion about what it means to be a good Muslim. At a conference I organised in 2009 under the umbrella of LUCIS, scholars presented an array of statements by medieval Muslims which appear unorthodox and even subversive – statements, for example, that the fasting month of Ramadan, rather than bringing joy and satisfaction, as the conventional view would have it, is a time of miserable abstinence and denial. But these views are not necessarily merely delinquent or contrarian. God's word revealed to Muhammad as recorded in the Qur'an generated an immense exegetic literature by historians, grammarians, jurists, theologians and other scholars. It is now generally agreed that a complete copy of the Qur'an was in circulation at least by A.D. 700.[3] The first *tafsīr*s, Qur'anic commentaries, already appeared at the beginning of the eighth century and new ones continue to appear up until today. These contemporary commentaries, which are not always in traditional forms, partially restate opinions of older authorities but also often add their own dramatically differing views as well.[4] With the appearance of the earliest commentaries a debate arose about the legitimacy of composing such commentaries at all. And while certain early authorities, such as the companions and earliest followers of Muhammad, are considered by *all* worthy of citation and respect, different political and religious groups chose their own additional authorities. Qur'anic commentaries consequently differ in some fundamental ways, depending on the religious and/or political outlook of the author.

Similarly, the body of sayings and deeds of Muhammad (Sunna) that serves as a guidebook to Muslims contains many conflicting views on fundamental issues. Opposing opinions as voiced by different authorities are mentioned side by side by the medieval collectors of the *hadiths* as they tended to be more interested in reliability, based on verifiable chains of transmission, than in the contents of these reports.

In the same way, although Islamic law according to classical Islamic thought is the revealed will of God, not made by society but an eternally valid ideal to which society is to aspire and as such unchanging and ahistorical, the discovery and formulation of the divine law is a continuous process.[5] Islamic legal texts contain a wide variety of different arguments and precepts and we even see that a special legal literary genre listing different opinions about one and the same topic arose, the so-called *ikhtilaf* works. In these works the opinions of the different *madhhab*s, Islamic law schools, and of key-jurists belonging to these schools were listed next to each other. It is now clear that individuals (Muslims and non-Muslims) living under Islam were well aware of these differences between the Islamic law schools and exploited them to their advantage.[6] Especially in the realm of Islamic family law – the rules governing marriage and divorce – substantial differences exist between the different law schools, which has led to opinion-shopping from the medieval to the contemporary period. In a more extreme context, Shi'ite inheritance law offers fathers the possibility to pass a larger share of their inheritance to their daughters than Sunni law, motivating some parents to convert for this reason alone.[7]

These are the products of an ongoing debate between believers over the correct response of Muslim dogma to an endlessly complex reality. The absence of a central doctrinal legislator in Islam ensures that dogma remains perennially open to interpretation and discussion.[8] In this 'marketplace' of ideas and opinions every believer is in principle a trader. As such, there always have been – and very likely always will be – a diversity of opinions about what constitutes Islam and correct Islamic behaviour. Muslim communities are not uniform and unchanging.

The Origin and Development of Islam in Historical and Academic Research Can Be Studied without Calling Islamic Beliefs into Question

Research into the origins of Islam has become politically sensitive, as the scholar Tom Holland put it: It is 'a topic that is currently more mired in controversy than any other in the entire field of ancient history.'[9] In the current debate, the amount of administrative experience, political know-how and cultural sophistication that the Arab armies brought with them in their seventh-century conquests is often confused with the question of the originality and uniqueness of Islam as a religion. The lack of conformity between the Qur'an that we know from printed editions available now in the Middle East and the one known from manuscript fragments from the first century of Islam has been used to argue for a lack of unity in the earliest Muslim revelations or even a total nonexistence. The absence of detailed descriptions of Muslim religious rituals in contemporary non-Muslim sources has led some scholars to argue for the coming into existence of Islam at a much later moment and a different place than seventh-century Arabia. On the one hand, findings that appear to confirm the traditional Muslim version of Islamic history by according a major role to the Prophet and the early Muslim community in the Arabian Peninsula are quickly interpreted as naïve endorsements of the Muslim agenda. On the other, research that indicates borrowings by early Muslims from subject societies is often interpreted as condescending to Islam and, to the degree to which it appears to challenge Islam's truth claims, politically hostile.

Another topic where the study of early Islamic history is drawn into and distorted by the contemporary debate is the discussion concerning the inherent peaceful or violent nature of Islam. A recently published book discussing early Islam as an inclusive movement that allowed Jews and Christians to join without converting and not intent on imposing its Muslim beliefs on non-believers has received a lot of attention from adherents of both sides.[10] On the one side it has been described to speak to those hankering for a 'nice, tolerant and open Islam.'[11] On the other end of the spectrum the author's representation of Muslims not intending to impose their beliefs by force is considered a wishful and politically motivated, fabulous reconstruction of what is in reality one 'irredeemably violent Islam'. The formation of Islam is characterised by the many different ideas and viewpoints which were continuously expressed, fought and put aside either because they lacked appeal to believers or because stronger parties in society successfully got rid of them – often in a very violent manner. This scholarly observation is not the same as seeing Islam as one ever liberal and open-minded religion of peace. It also does not follow that one accepts the view that since a multiform medieval period 'a tolerant Islam was hijacked by extremists'.[12] It emphasises, rather, the need to consider and try to understand *all* the different views that played a role in Islamic and Muslims' thought throughout the centuries. Not only because it is necessary to show both Muslims and non-Muslims the diversity and space for argument that this religion has allowed for and should continue to allow for, but because of academic integrity.

The heat needs to be drawn from this debate: we need historical-critical research to continue to probe into this crucial period of Islam without ideological interference. We should aim for a situation in which we do not constantly need to explain that disinterested historical inquiry has no bearing on the force and validity of Islam as a faith. There is simply too much at stake for it to be otherwise.

Notes

1   See the saying attributed to Muhammad, 'Whoever dies without recognising the Imam of his age dies the death of a pagan.'

2   Those following the right imam by contrast were called *ahl al-janna*, the people of paradise (P. Crone, *God's Rule: Government and Islam*, New York: Columbia University Press; 2004, p. 22).

3   See most recently F. Déroche, *Le codex Parisino-petropolitanus* (Leiden/Boston: E.J. Brill; 2009).

4   See especially the so-called 'feminist commentaries' as discussed by K. Bauer '*The Male Is Not Like the Female* (Q 3:36): The Question of Gender Egalitarianism in the Qur'an', *Religion Compass* 3-4 (2009): p. 637-654. See also the work of the Syrian thinker Muhammad Shahrur (b. 1938), the Egyptian Mahmud Shaltut (1893-1963) and Muhammad Hussein Fadlallah (1935-2010). I am very grateful to Karen Bauer for sharing her knowledge on this topic with me.

5   See for example W. Hallaq on the debate whether the process of legal reasoning and judgement (*ijtihad*) was ever abolished in Islamic law: 'Was the Gate of Ijtihad Closed?', *International Journal of Middle East Studies* 16 (1984): p. 3-41.

6   See for example for the medieval period: Y. Rapoport, 'Legal Diversity in the Age of *Taqlīd*: The Four Chief Qadis under the Mamluks', *Islamic Law and Society* 10/2 (2003), p. 210-228 and for the contemporary period: 'Shopping for Legal Forums: Christians and Family Law in Modern Egypt,' in: *Dispensing Justice in Islam: Qadis and their Judgments*, eds. Khaled Masud, Ruud Peters & David Powers (Leiden: Brill; 2006; p. 451-469).

7   For these differences, see N.J. Coulson, *Succession in the Muslim Family* (Cambridge: Cambridge University Press; 1971). I am thankful to Robert Gleave for this reference and his willingness to discuss this issue with me.

8   Even the idea that after the formative period of Islamic law, up to ca. 900, independent legal interpretation was no longer possible (the closing of the gates of *ijtihad*) having been replaced by explanation, application and interpretation of doctrine (*taqlīd*) (cf. J. Schacht, *An Introduction to Islamic Law*, Oxford: Oxford University Press; 1964, chapter 10) has been criticised (e.g. W. Hallaq, 'Was the Gate of Ijtihad Closed?', *International Journal of Middle East Studies* 16 (1984): p. 3-41).

9   Tom Holland, ancient historian and author on the discussion forum *No More Crusades* (accessed 30 March 2011).

10 Fred Donner, *Muhammad and the Believers: At the Origins of Islam* (Boston: Harvard University Press; 2010).

11 Patricia Crone in a review of Fred Donner's book in *Tablet Magazine* on-line publication (posted 10 August 2010).

12 See Jonah Goldberg's column of 07 January 2011 (accessed 17 August 2011: http:// townhall.com/columnists/jonahgoldberg/2011/01/07/ islams_hijackers_and_hijackees.

Islamic Studies in the Dutch Public Sphere

Léon Buskens

With Islam dominating the headlines, academia could gain from the heightened public attention to Islam, which offers new opportunities for Dutch researchers. At the same time, a close relationship between scholarly activity and public demands calls for a critical reflection.

In the past three decades, there has been an unprecedented growth in national and international scholarship about Islam and Muslims. This can, in the first place, be concluded from the sheer amount of publications and graduations on the topic, but also from the rise in academic centres focusing on Islam. In the Netherlands several university departments for the study of the Middle East and Arabic were converted into centres for Islamic studies with a strong focus on Islam in the West. Moreover, new institutes were established specifically for the pursuance of Islamic studies. Examples are the ISIM (International Institute for the Study of Islam in the Modern World: 1998-2009), which was unfortunately closed, LUCIS (the Leiden University Centre for the Study of Islam and Society, set up in 2009) and NISIS (Netherlands Interuniversity School for Islamic Studies, set up in 2010 by eight Dutch universities and supported by the Dutch Ministry of Education, Culture and Science).

The increasing academic interest in the study of Islam links in with multiple developments. Here I will focus on the increasing need in our society for knowledge about Islam and Muslims. During the last three decades, the study of Islam as a practical science has seen a revival since the colonial period, when European administrators governed large parts of the Islamic world. Oil-dependency in the West and the Iranian Revolution of 1979 were incentives for the study of Islam outside Europe. Governments and people have presented themselves increasingly as Muslims. Since the 1970s, a similar trend can be observed among Mediterranean immigrants in West-Europe, who are now in the first place Muslims rather than migrant workers, both in their own eyes as in the eyes of Dutch society.

The end of the Cold War, according to some intellectuals, also marked the end of history. Remarkably, Muslims once again became the ultimate 'Other', enemies of the West, which fitted with a century-old tradition of mutual stereotyping. At the start of the 1990s, the Dutch politician Frits Bolkestein framed Islam as an issue of political concern through a series of speeches and newspaper articles. The 9/11 attacks reinforced the idea that Islam forms a 'problem', for which a solution is needed.[1]

Essentialism

Major changes in the practice of Islamic studies at Dutch universities over the last few decades are immediately apparent. The presence of second- and third-generation Muslim migrants has led to an increased number of university students who have first-hand knowledge of the languages and cultures of the Islamic world. The presence of Muslim students can sometimes influence teaching, when they resist certain critical and analytical readings of history. Not all students favour a critical-historical approach to the beginnings of Islam, or an agnostic approach which considers Islam as a cultural phenomenon among many others.

In Dutch universities the focus in research and teaching has shifted from 'Islam' to 'Muslim societies' and from a philological to a social-science approach.[2] Indeed, the strong criticism of traditional Middle-Eastern and Islamic studies, which Edward Said so clearly expressed in his *Orientalism* (1978), has, with some delay, also made its impact in the Netherlands.[3]

Present academic studies tend to emphasise the diversity and complexity of Islamic societies. In fact, there are now few scholars who still embrace an essentialist approach to Islam. Characterising other cultures by referring to a fixed dominant core is no longer regarded as scientific. In the Netherlands, particularly the anthropological study of Muslims has flourished, notably in Nijmegen and Amsterdam – both at the Free University and the University of Amsterdam.[4] The research programme of ISIM further incentivised the anthropological approach.[5]

Gradually, Islam as the religion actually practised by Muslims in the Netherlands became a topic of interest for academics both in social sciences and religious studies. Whilst in the early 1980s, religion hardly played a role in the study of migrant communities, it now has become a prime feature. We now possess a series of important doctoral theses and monographs about Islam in the Netherlands. The University of Amsterdam, the Free University (in Amsterdam), Utrecht University and Leiden University offer degree programmes on Islam in the West.

All this knowledge seems to see little dissemination outside academic circles. Public opinion is being dominated by non-experts, whether positively or negatively inclined. This article will address the latter, as they dominate the public debate with opinions which are often miles apart from the views of most academic Islam experts.[6]

Among the Dutch critics of Islam, those who have 'personally experienced' Islam, often draw much attention. Their negative views are persuasive to many as their strong rhetoric is supposedly supported by first-hand experience. The best-known representatives from this group are Afshin Ellian and Ayaan Hirsi Ali. They have constructed a conflict between Islamic and Western values, built on a range of generalising and oversimplified statements. Their personal experiences offer an endless source of opinions, mixed in with an underlying sentiment of populism. The Manichean outline of Samuel Huntington's *Clash of Civilisations* structures their discourse.

A second group consists of eloquent professors and public intellectuals who have been trained in normative analysis, for example through degrees in jurisprudence and philosophy, without having much knowledge about Islam. This group includes people such as Paul Cliteur, Herman Philipse and Paul Scheffer. They hold Bernard Lewis' later writings in high esteem. However, the new generation of Islam researchers is particularly critical of this work of the aged emeritus professor of Princeton University for its essentialist nature.[7]

A third group of Islam critics consists of politicians, such as Frits Bolkestein, Pim Fortuyn, Geert Wilders and Martin Bosma. They spread a negative image of Islam and Muslims in a very vocal way. Bolkestein is the only one of the four who has seriously studied some of the academic literature, though his choice of readings remains quite selective.

The only academic with a formal training in Islamic studies backing these 'Islam bashers' is Hans Jansen, a former colleague in Leiden, now emeritus professor of Utrecht University. He has published numerous books and is well versed in media appearances. A wide audience, notably those with a general dislike of Islam, considers him as *the* expert on Islam. Jansen frequently opposes what he considers 'trendy developments' in his research area. He prefers philology to the social sciences, admires the work of Bernard Lewis and regards Edward Said as a false prophet. His academic approach tends to be essentialist. Since the 1990s, concern about violence in Islamic movements has increasingly played a role in his work. Wilders has often justified his vision of Islam by referring to Jansen's publications, as evidence of the truth about Islam.

Fear

The public image of Islam in the Netherlands is greatly influenced by the essentialist views and fears of these opinion leaders. When academics on the basis of empirical research argue that not all Muslims in the Netherlands adhere to one monolithic Islam and warn against spreading fear, these public figures often respond with insinuations and reproaches of not telling *the* truth about *the* Islam. Perhaps this widespread need for an essentialist perspective of the Muslim 'enemy' is simply a local and temporary manifestation of a universal phenomenon, i.e. the need for stereotyping 'the other' in order to ascertain one's own values. Many historical studies show that for centuries Muslims have been the 'bad neighbours', who provide Europeans with a mirror image to define themselves, and vice versa.[8] As a form of 'alterity' the so-called 'Occidentalism' as can be found in many Muslim countries, is no different from orientalism.[9]

Putting the present debate in a historical and comparative perspective, however, does not make the public need for information about Islam and Muslims any less urgent. The government has assigned dozens of research projects, both directly through ministries or indirectly through NGOs, research councils and the police, in order to obtain reliable knowledge. Recent research topics include arranged marriages, honour killings, polygamy, unofficial 'Islamic' marriages and Muslim youth culture. Remarkably, most of these projects are carried out by legal scholars or sociologists, who have no specialist knowledge about Islam and Muslims. Is such specialist knowledge not important, or do Islam researchers hide their light under a bushel?

In my view, researchers should take public responsibility and actively pursue policy-relevant research assignments. The insights which researchers have obtained during the past few decades can prove to be of great value and indeed bear much practical relevance for society. By presenting the Dutch public with an anti-essentialist image of complex, diverse and context-dependent perceptions and practices of Islam, researchers can raise the level of the public debate and become a useful resource for policymakers and politicians.

Integrity

My argument is not that academic study should only respond to public demands. Scholars should continue doing research for intellectual gratification. Yet, we have to remember that scholarly work receives public funding because society expects the results to be useful and applicable. The academic study of Islam arose in Leiden and Delft in the nineteenth century for the purpose of training civil servants to govern the Dutch East-Indies.[10] Other European colonial powers saw similar trends. After independence of the colonies this type of knowledge suddenly seemed to have lost its practical significance. The importance of oil and large-scale Muslim immigration revived the interest in the study of Islam and Muslim societies. Instead of denying the impact of these factors on academia, we should rather make them a topic of analysis. Three areas ask for further consideration.

First, we need to pay careful attention to the relationship between academic knowledge, normative positions and policymaking. Analytically and intellectually, these domains can be separated; each domain requires its own training and skills. The debate on Islam in the Netherlands would benefit from interactions between these domains. For example, Islam researchers know much about Muslims, yet often are not trained to make normative judgements about their findings. They ought to consider systematically the assumptions and social circumstances informing their research. Legal scholars and philosophers are trained to make normative judgements, balancing conflicting values. They can explain an educated audience how to appreciate different views. Finally, it is up to the politicians to decide which position the government takes, and how certain norms and values feed into policy. Such choices and decisions inevitably involve a degree of arbitrariness; normative decisions often cannot be fully rationalised. However, there are many ways in which we can make the debates about these choices more rational, by emphasising the three-fold approach, and by considering and discussing each step carefully and openly. I am fully aware that this will be difficult to realise in practice, if only because of the fact that such normative issues often go hand in hand with emotions running high.

Second, we should consider the complex relationship between academic freedom and research commissioned by governments and other interested institutions. Academic integrity has been much debated over the last few years, partly because those who commission research can have an interest in a particular outcome. Whereas research ethics require that researchers prioritise the interests of those who are being investigated, this could conflict with the goals of the commissioner, for example when it concerns topics such as radicalisation and terrorism.

In this respect the history of our research area offers an important lesson. As said, the origin of Islamic studies is closely related to European expansion and the economic and political interests involved. The discussions held in the 1970s and 1980s about the life, work and morals of Christiaan Snouck Hurgronje (1857-1936), who was a Dutch colonial government advisor between 1889 and 1905, present an interesting case. The reputation of Snouck Hurgronje turned from an intellectual hero and a great man into an immoral scoundrel through the close link between his academic work and the bloody colonial politics. His opportunism and his research methods ethically appeared below the standards of the late twentieth century. His reluctance to acknowledge the important role of key informants in his field work, his tendency to change religious identity depending on the context and his marriages to two Javanese women aroused much criticism.[11] Of course, at the start of the twenty-first century our own research is also informed by its social settings. This calls for a critical reflection of such influences on our findings and on the ways in which we study Muslims and Islam.[12]

Third, we should reflect on the presentation of our research findings as well as on the description and creation of images of Islam and Muslims, the so-called *representation*. After all, there is a narrow connection between form and content, and presentation is vital for conveying our findings effectively. Why is it that serious studies on Islam get so little access to the media? Why does the audience at academic gatherings so often consist of the same like-minded people? Should scholars consider alternative ways to convey their messages? Does the secret lie in media training? Should researchers seek closer cooperation with science journalists and what are the ramifications of such collaborations for their work? Should academics rather than respond to public debates and opinions, actively seek the spotlight to present their own research findings?

Most of my Dutch colleagues know from their own experience how difficult it is to attract public attention to detailed knowledge and nuanced opinions about Islam and Muslims. The Dutch media, as in most other countries, often opt for *oneliners*, preferably with a negative connotation. Yet, it does not help to feel wronged and complain that our messages are not welcomed. Seeking access into the mass media in order to disseminate our knowledge remains an important challenge.

In addition, it may well pay off to look for alternative forms of publicity. Cooperation with museums could be a fruitful and appealing way to bring research findings to the attention of a broader public. The successful exhibitions about Muslim cultures in De Nieuwe Kerk and Tropenmuseum (both in Amsterdam) are excellent examples. The curator of the Middle-East department of the Tropenmuseum, Mirjam Shatanawi, made a significant contribution to the debate on representation through her book *Islam in beeld* [Islam in Images] (2009).[13]

Increased cooperation between academics in the Netherlands could contribute substantially to greater visibility in the Islam debate. Hopefully the recently established LUCIS as a centre of expertise at Leiden University and the national network of NISIS, which unites specialists on Islam and Muslim societies at eight Dutch universities, offer incentives to Dutch researchers for a fruitful debate and cooperation. Both initiatives further the awareness that research on Islam can be of relevance for Dutch society and at the same time also contribute to the international scholarly debate on the comparative study of Muslim societies in the past and the present.

Notes

1   For overviews of the Dutch debate on Islam in English, see: Ian Buruma, *Murder in Amsterdam. The Death of Theo van Gogh and the Limits of Tolerance* (London: Atlantic Books; 2006); and Peter van der Veer, 'Pim Fortuyn, Theo van Gogh, and the Politics of Tolerance in the Netherlands', in *Public Culture* 18 (2006) no. 1, p. 111-124. For the sake of comparison it is important to look at studies of similar debates in other European countries, such as: Unni Wikan, *Generous Betrayal. Politics of Culture in the New Europe* (Chicago: The University of Chicago Press; 2002); and two monographs by John R. Bowen, *Why the French Don't Like Headscarves. Islam, the State, and Public Space* (Princeton & Oxford: Princeton University Press; 2007) and *Can Islam be French? Pluralism and Pragmatism in a Secularist State* (Princeton & Oxford: Princeton University Press; 2010).

2   For example, see the contributions in the special edition of *Sharqiyyât* 15 (2003) no. 1-2, '25 jaar Midden-Oosten en islamstudies in Nederland en de MOI', which appeared on the occasion of the 25th anniversary of the Dutch Association for Middle Eastern and Islamic Studies; and Léon Buskens, 'Vanishing Orientalism in Leiden', *ISIM Review* no. 18 (2006), p. 44-45. An international context for the changes in Islamic studies is offered by the volume edited by Carl W. Ernst & Richard C. Martin, *Rethinking Islamic Studies. From Orientalism to Cosmopolitanism* (Columbia, South Carolina: The University of South Carolina Press; 2010). Examples of case studies that result from this social-science turn in Islamic studies can be found in the volume edited by Miriam Cooke & Bruce B. Lawrence, *Muslim Networks from Hajj to Hip Hop* (Chapel Hill & London: The University of North Carolina Press; 2005). A critical review of the contemporary predicament of Islamic studies and its social context by German colleagues is presented in Abbas Poya & Maurus Reinkowski (eds.) *Das Unbehagen in der Islamwissenschaft. Ein klassisches Fach im Scheinwerferlicht der Politik und der Medien* (Bielefeld: Transcript; 2007).

3   Maxime Robinson was invited to Nijmegen University in 1976 to give a critical review of Middle Eastern and Islamic studies, which was consequently published under the name *La fascination de L'islam. Etapes du regard occidental sur le monde musulman* in the MOI collected essays no. 2 (1978). A revised and expanded version of this lecture appeared in 1981 (Paris: François Maspero). Jacques Waardenburg offered an early critical analysis of Islamic studies in his doctoral thesis *L'Islam dans le miroir de l'Occident* (The Hague & Paris: Mouton; 1963, 2nd edition). Peter van der Veer elaborated on the critique of orientalism from the United States for a Dutch audience in his collection *Modern oriëntalisme. Essays over de westerse beschavingsdrang* (Amsterdam: Meulenhoff; 1995). For some time Leiden scholars seemed to prefer the views of Bernard Lewis, yet thanks to the efforts of Pieter Sjoerd van Koningsveld, Edward Said was eventually invited to give an impressive lecture in front of a select audience. Van Koningsveld published in collaboration with Wasif Shadid a series of studies on the representation of the Islam, both in the past and present. For an overview, refer to chapter 1 'Westerse beeldvorming over de islam' in P.S. van Koningsveld, *Sprekend over de islam en de moderne tijd*, (Utrecht: Stichting Teleac/Amsterdam: Prometheus; 1993).

4   For an overview of the Dutch contributions to the anthropology of Muslim societies, see article of Léon Buskens and Ruud Strijp, 'Antropologische studies in het Midden-Oosten en van de islam: een overzicht van 25 jaar onderzoek in Nederland', in *Sharqiyyât* 15 (2003) no. 1-2, p. 149-198.

5   Unfortunately, only few scholars have as yet paid attention to the historical perspective on the study of day-to-day Islam, i.e. the way in which people interpret Islam according to the specific social context.

6 Opinion leaders spreading a positive view, such as Job Cohen, Geert Mak and Sjoerd de Jong, are not Islam specialists either.

7 The early works of Bernard Lewis did not escape criticism either, for example during the oration of Erik-Jan Zürcher, the speech he gave upon entering the professorship of Turkisch studies at Leiden University, entitled *Opkomst en ondergang van het 'moderne' Turkije* (Leiden: Onderzoeksschool CNWS; 1998). In this lecture Zürcher gave a critical reflection on one of the Lewis' most famous books, *The Emergence of Modern Turkey* (1961).

8 The classical account of the history of the European views of Islam is offered by Norman Daniel in his two books, *Islam and the West. The Making of an Image* (Edinburgh: The University Press; 1960) and *Islam, Europe and Empire* (Edinburgh: At the University Press; 1966). The standard account of orientalist scholarship is Johann Fück, *Die arabischen Studien in Europa. Bis in den Anfang des 20. Jahrhunderts* (Leipzig: Otto Harrassowitz; 1955). Robert Irwin intended to refute Edward Said's critical analysis of orientalist scholarship with his *For Lust of Knowing. The Orientalists and their Enemies* (London: Allen Lane; 2006). A recent overview of both the scholarly and popular traditions, with further references, is offered by Zachary Lockmann, *Contending Visions of the Middle East. The History and Politics of Orientalism* (Cambridge: Cambridge University Press; 2010; second edition).

9 See for example Ian Buruma & Avishai Margalit, *Occidentalism. A Short History of Anti-Westernism* (New York: Penguin Books; 2004); and Robert Woltering, *Occidentalisms. Images of 'the West' in Egypt* (Leiden: PhD Thesis; 2009).

10 An impressive overview of the Dutch colonial Islam study with an excellent introduction can be found in B.J. Boland & I. Farjon, *Islam in Indonesia. A Bibliographical Survey 1600-1942 with post-1945 Addenda* (Dordrecht: Foris Publications Holland; 1983). For specific research into the origins of the study of Islamic law in the Netherlands: Léon Buskens, 'Twee negentiende eeuwse ontdekkers van het Islamitisch recht te Delft. Een begin van het debat over theorie en praktijk', in Paulien van der Grinten & Ton Heukels (eds.); *Crossing Borders. Essays in European and Private International Law, Nationality Law and Islamic Law in Honour of Frans van der Velden*; (Deventer: Kluwer; 2005; p. 153-171 + bibliography); and Léon Buskens & Jean Kommers, 'The Delayed Reception of Colonial Studies about Adat Law and Islamic Law in Dutch Anthropology', in Han Vermeulen & Jean Kommers (eds.), *Tales from Academia. History of Anthropology in the Netherlands* (Saarbrücken: Verlag für Entwicklungspolitik Saarbrücken GmbH; 2002; p. 733-755).

11 For example, see Pieter Sjoerd van Koningsveld, *Snouck Hurgronje en de Islam. Acht artikelen over leven en werk van een oriëntalist uit het koloniale tijdperk* (Leiden: Documentatiebureau Islam-Christendom; 1987); and the introduction of Jan Just Witkam to his translation of Christiaan Snouck Hurgronje's *Mekka in de tweede helft van de negentiende eeuw. Schetsen uit het dagelijks leven* (Amsterdam/Antwerpen: Atlas; 2007).

12 A reflection of the anthropological representation of Islam is offered by Daniel M. Varisco, *Islam Obscured. The Rhetoric of Anthropological Representation* (New York: Palgrave Macmillan; 2005).

13 Mirjam Shatanawi, *Islam in beeld. Kunst en cultuur van moslims wereldwijd* (Amsterdam: SUN; 2009).

'Taki-What? What Are You Talking About?'[1]

Maurits Berger

The assumption that Muslims hide their true intentions – the concept known as *takiyya* – is ludicrous. Most Muslims do not even know that this phenomenon exists.

In 2011, the leader of the Dutch Party of Freedom (PVV), Geert Wilders, successfully challenged the impartiality of the Amsterdam Court judges who were hearing the case against Wilders for inciting hatred and discrimination of Muslims. But back in his seat as parliamentarian several days later he did exactly the very thing he had been accused of because, according to Mr Wilders, Muslims in the Netherlands were guilty of practising *takiyya*.

Takiyya originates from the Shia doctrine of Islam, and means the dissimulation of one's religion. This dogma was developed in two different forms: one was that dissimulation could be necessary if one was threatened or persecuted for one's religious convictions, and the other was that a unique set of knowledge about one's religion had to be kept secret.

At present, this dogmatic concept has lost its relevance. One of the exceptions is the small Shia sect of the Druze in the Middle East – for them, adaptation to their environment and secrecy of religious knowledge has continued to play an important role in their religious and social life.

So why the sudden interest of a Dutch parliamentarian in this term and what is its relevance to Muslims in the West? It turns out that some Western authors in recent publications on Islam in the West have brought up *takiyya*. They warned that however friendly Muslims may appear, in fact they simply try to fool us. According to these authors, Muslims cover up their real intentions, which basically consist of destroying the perverse West and replacing it with an Islamic state.

What do these authors base their opinions on? Because given the fact that the overall majority of Muslims in the West adhere to Sunni Islam, it seems awkward to refer to the Shia doctrine of *takiyya*, which, by the way, is rejected by Sunni doctrine. It turns out that these authors mostly refer to each other.

But their primary source can be traced to the writings of a few Islamic extremists who prescribe that a sensible terrorist in practising jihad should cover up his or her real intentions in order to avoid suspicion. So rather than wearing the obligatory beard and jellaba they should walk around cleanly shaven in three-piece suits. Such advice is hardly surprising: there are few terrorists who do not hide their identity. And in the case of a jihad extremist, such recommendations will be phrased in Islamic jargon. Reference to a Shia concept like *takiyya* then serves the purpose.

But should we suspect *all* Muslims of *takiyya*? Ironically, very few Muslims both in the Muslim and Western world know of this notion. Questioning Muslims in the West results in a confused gaze: What are you talking about? Taki-what?

Yet, in the view of Mr Wilders and his supporters, such a denial merely strengthens the suspicion of *takiyya*, for is it not the very purpose of that notion to pretend ignorance? This puts Muslims in an impossible position. They can never prove that they do not practise *takiyya*, because every denial becomes a positive confirmation. It is as if they would say: 'I am not a liar'. This logic makes the accusation of *takiyya* a slow but very effective poison. For how can Muslims – any Muslim – be trusted anymore?

It is shocking that quite some people in the Netherlands now appear to believe that *takiyya* is an important aspect of Islam – not specifically of a small Shia community, but of all Muslims globally. During lectures in remote villages I have been confronted with questions on this totally obscure dogmatic practice with roots in medieval Shia doctrine: 'But sir, Muslims practise *takiyya*, don't they?' A similar line of reasoning would be to refer to the practice of witch trials in medieval Europe, whereby only drowning was sufficient proof that the woman was no witch: since most European women can swim, they must be witches, right?

The use of Islamic terminology snatched from their theological and historical contexts is a recent and recurring phenomenon in Western discourse on Islam. The Dutch parliament has witnessed plenary discussions on topics like 'jihad', 'salafism', 'sharia' – and now it is *takkiya*. But this time the implications are much more serious.

The fact that Mr Wilders is now using this in parliament makes me want to quote his own words: has he gone utterly mad?[2] Firstly, why this preposterous abuse of theological terminology, of which he has obviously no idea, if not to serve his political interests? Secondly, how does he dare – from his position in parliament, during a plenary session and in front of the cameras – accuse Muslims en masse of not being trustworthy and potentially undermining or threatening the state?

I was sceptical about the court case against Mr Wilders in the first place – not because Mr Wilders would not be insulting towards

Muslims (that he is), but because I do not think that it is sensible to criminalise critique on a religion. The *takiyya* discussion, however, goes way beyond criticising religious doctrines. Accusing Muslims without any ground of practising *takiyya* is tantamount to discrimination and incitement of hatred against Muslims.

Notes

1   This is an elaborated version of an opinion article published in the Dutch daily *NRC Handelsblad* of 28 October 2010.
2   These were the words used by Wilders in his reaction to the Secretary of State of Residence, Suburbs and Integration when she remarked that in the future we might very well speak of the Netherlands as a Christian-Jewish-Humanist-Islamic culture ('Have you gone utterly mad?' – *Bent u knettergek geworden?*).

Sharia and Law in a Bird's-Eye View: Reform, Moderation and Ambiguity

Jan Michiel Otto

Over the last three decades my area of research has been law and governance in developing countries. I have been particularly interested in the formation and development of legal systems in these countries, the way these systems operate in practice and the influence on governance and socio-economic development. As a researcher of law and governance, I studied local administration in rural areas of Indonesia or Egypt. One inevitably comes into contact with Islam and Islamic law, even if this is not the main research objective. For example, Islamic law became a prominent issue during my field research in Egypt in 1980, because the Egyptian constitution underwent a significant change in Article 2 from stating that 'sharia is *a* source of law' to 'sharia is *the* source of law'. In this way Sadat tried to regain the support of the Muslim conservatives. He had distanced himself by promulgating a progressive marriage law and by pacifying relations with Israel. At the time many wondered whether the constitutional change would influence other areas of law, such as criminal law. However, the next thirty years show that criminal law did not become strongly islamised. Did family law become more conservative as a consequence of the 1980 constitutional revision? The answer is no. Several critics including Rudolph Peters have recounted the way in which the government and its allies in parliament prevented this from happening. In fact, the Egyptian government first led by Sadat and later by Mubarak, made efforts to liberalise family law. By introducing the *khul'*-law in 2000 it eventually managed to do so.

Indonesia provides a second suitable example. During the last few decades the issue of sharia has drawn much attention, for example there have been questions about the Islamic character of the 1974 marriage law, which limits polygamy and repudiation and subjects cases to approval by the Islamic courts. There were debates about the broadening of the jurisdiction of these courts through a law in 1989. Further issues included the different legal position that Aceh received in 2001, which led to provincial regulations with Islamic criminal provisions.

Inspired by these observations, the idea arose to undertake a comparative study about sharia and national law. In collaboration with a group of international experts and on request of the Scientific Council for Government Policy (WRR) in the Netherlands, we started the project in 2004. The following countries were selected: Afghanistan, Egypt, Indonesia, Iran, Malaysia, Mali, Morocco, Nigeria, Pakistan, Saudi Arabia, Sudan and Turkey.

In these countries we did research into the development of the legal systems over the following four consecutive periods. We chose 1800 until 1920 as the first period. We labelled this period as the time of colonialism and European expansion. The second period runs from 1920 until 1965. This period is marked by state formation, an emphasis on national unification, decline of religion and tradition for the sake of 'development', liberal ideologies moving to socialism returning to liberal ideologies and a period of undemocratic regimes. The next period was decided to run from 1965 until 1985. In these twenty years, many countries saw authoritarianism followed by economic and political liberalisation. Tradition and religion reappeared. This period was also marked by the Iranian Revolution of 1979, the introduction of Islamic criminal law in Pakistan and Numeiri's introduction of sharia in Sudan (1983/1984). The final period in the study starts in 1985 and lasts until the present day. In this period we see a mixed picture. On the one hand, there is a revival of Islam, whilst on the other hand one can witness an expansion of democracies and human rights movements. These years also see globalisation of Muslim terrorism with 9/11 as the prime example, an increase of military and ideological conflicts, yet stabilisation and liberalisation domestically.

We investigated the following three areas of law: constitutional law, family and inheritance law and criminal law. In each of these areas the countries face similar problems. With regards to constitutional law the issues at stake are the foundations of the state and the division of power. What is the country's *grundnorm*: the constitution or the sharia – the first principles of Islam? In particular, to what extent are basic human rights, included in the constitution, the ultimate points of reference? The issues of non-discrimination and freedom of religion require special attention. Who reviews sharia-based law against the constitution or vice versa? What role do the supreme judges play in this process? In terms of family and inheritance law the position of women holds a central place. The issues include polygamy, repudiation, right to divorce and share of inheritance. One of the central questions posed in this respect is to what extent the power balance between men and women, which according to the classical sharia favours the men, has been equalised by national law? With regards to criminal law, questions rise around crimes and punishments prescribed by classical sharia, followed by particular punishments: stoning in case of adultery, amputation in case of theft, flogging for the use of alcohol – punishments which most people would regard as inhumane nowadays. One of the most important conclusions of the study I would like to mention here:

> *Research into the legal systems of a cross sample of twelve Muslim countries shows that on the whole these countries in terms of women's rights, corporal punishment and democratisation have become more liberal over the past twenty years, and not, as many may have expected, more Islamic in a puritan sense.*

The country experts who contributed to the study were jurists, social scientists, area specialists and often combined all disciplines. Most of the experts were highly experienced in undertaking research in their particular country. The period in which we received the very first results was exciting. It was the first time that anyone had provided a full overview of the relation between sharia and national legal systems in the Muslim world. Soon it became clear that Saudi Arabia and Iran are exceptional cases in comparison with the other nine, more moderate countries and secular Turkey.

Besides Turkey's secular system, there are other constitutions of Muslim countries that do not refer to Islam explicitly, as is for example the case in Indonesia. The Nigerian constitution even forbids the introduction of an official national religion. Yet, most of the countries in the study are typically built on a dual foundation. The fundamental conflict that many Muslim countries face is because they have institutions that review bills against sharia and/or the constitution, such as the Constitutional Court and the Council of Guardians. Most governments also include a ministry of religion or religious affairs, which takes on the intermediary role between the religious authorities and the government. Such a ministry also supervises religious education, the mosques and the religious courts in order to guard the unity and integrity of the state. With regards to the judiciary, you often see that relatively moderate supreme courts overturn extreme sentences assigned by lower courts. An example is the case in North-Nigeria regarding the death sentence for Amina Lawal, which was fortunately never carried out. Similar developments have taken place in Pakistan.

The ambiguity within the legal systems reflects the fact that societies and individuals find themselves in a phase of transition with many traditional customs disappearing without effective new normative systems already in place. In a situation of instability and insecurity, 'multiple identity' flourishes, as does poly-normativism, legal pluralism, the informal sector and corruption. There is often a huge gap between law and practice. This applies both to the discrepancy between national law and social reality, and to the hiatus between classical sharia and daily practice.

It is worth noting that according to several of the country studies sharia and religious courts are frequently more woman-friendly and accessible than customary law and tribal chiefs prescribe. They even seem to surpass many state courts, which are hindered by red tape and corruption. It is the malfunctioning of state courts and perhaps also customary courts that explains the massive calls to support Islamic law in religious courts throughout the world. This leads to the second statement, which is also one of the conclusions of the study:

> *While the legal systems of most Muslim countries are fairly moderate when it comes to Islam and sharia, their constitutions are actually built on a dual foundation: the rule of law and Islam. This ambiguity legitimises the state, the law and the regime as well as the clergy, and it contributes to their peaceful coexistence. However, sometimes this ambiguity leaves the rule of law in a vulnerable position, failing to channel religious-political tensions.*

Whilst the Western ideological and religious spectrum is marked by believers versus secularists, the spectrum in the Muslim world ranges from puritan to moderate, whilst the support for a secular system is rather limited. The struggle between the puritans and the moderates in the Muslim world is one which has dominated its history, politics and the law for many centuries – an issue that the West knows too little about. Moderation practised by national governments with regards to the sharia is as old as the road to Mecca, and mainly flows from the practical demands of administration. The opposition of extreme Muslim puritans is usually directed against the moderation of its own leaders.

A considerable number of Muslim scholars have been championing the case of moderation. They evidently live by the ideals of social justice and human rights and are wary of strict dogmatism. Their striving for fairness and justice has much in common with similar ideas in the West, in spite of the different background. This brings me to the final proposition:

> *The sharia, as interpreted by pious and moderate Muslim scholars such as Khaled Abu el Fadl, Abdullahi An-Naim and the late Nurcholis Madjid, forms a useful source of inspiration for the promotion of human rights and the rule of law.*

Who Speaks for Islam? Learning What Most Muslims Think, and Some Lessons for Policymaking

Dalia Mogahed

Post-9/11 violence has grown exponentially as Muslims and non-Muslims alike continue to be victims of global terrorism. Terrorist attacks have occurred from Morocco to Indonesia and from Madrid to London, and wars in Afghanistan and Iraq rage on. Is all this evidence of an all-out clash or war between the West and 1.3 billion Muslims? The vital missing piece among the many voices weighing in on this question is the actual views of everyday Muslims. With all that is at stake for the West and Muslim societies, indeed for the world's future, it is time to democratise the debate.

Who Speaks for Islam? What a Billion Muslims Really Think[1] is about this *silenced* majority. This book is the product of a mammoth, multi-year Gallup research study. Between 2001 and 2007, Gallup conducted tens of thousands of hour-long, face-to-face interviews with residents of more than 35 nations that are predominantly Muslim or have substantial Muslim populations. The sample represents residents, young and old, educated and illiterate, female and male, and from urban and rural settings. With the random sampling method that Gallup used, results are statistically valid within a plus or minus 3-point margin of error. In totality, we surveyed a sample representing more than 90% of the world's 1.3 billion Muslims, making this the largest, most comprehensive study of contemporary Muslims ever done. This vast amount of data represents the views of the world's Muslims, revealing answers to the questions everyone is asking: What is the root of anti-Americanism in the Muslim world? Who are the extremists? Do Muslims desire democracy, and if so, what might it look like? What do Muslim women really want? The concept of this book is simple: with these questions in hand, we let the statistical evidence – the voices of a billion Muslims, not individual 'experts' or 'extremists' – dictate the answer. The results often challenge conventional wisdom.

Gallup's research produced a number of insights, but the most important was this: the conflict between the Muslim and Western communities is far from inevitable. It is more about policy than princi-ples. However, until and unless decision makers listen directly to the people and gain an accurate understanding of this conflict, extremists on all sides will continue to gain ground. Our data revealed far more than what we could possibly cover in one book, so we chose the most significant, and at times, surprising conclusions to share with the read-er. Today, I will touch upon some of the most important findings re-garding Muslim-West relations, the role of women and radicalisation.

Why Do They Hate Us?

Shortly after 9/11, George W. Bush declared in a national address: 'Americans are asking, why do they hate us? They hate what we see right here in this chamber – a democratically elected government. Their leaders are self-appointed. They hate our freedoms – our freedom of religion, our freedom of speech, our freedom to vote and assemble and disagree with each other.' Yet despite widespread anti-American and anti-British sentiment, Muslims around the world said they, in fact, admired much of what the West holds dear. When asked to describe what they admired most about the West in an open-ended question, the most frequent response was technology, expertise and knowledge; the second most frequent was freedom and democracy. When Americans were asked the same question in fact, the top two responses were identical.

To give you just a flavour of the responses:

'Freedom of the press, opinion and expression. Also, scientific advancement.'

– Saudi respondent

'Social justice and having access to nuclear power. Real democracy.'

– Iranian respondent

'Law is above all and everyone observes the law.'

– Pakistani respondent

'Their political system is transparent and they are following democracy in its true sense.'

– Pakistani respondent

'Liberty and freedom and being open-minded with each other.'

– Moroccan respondent

Contrary to what might be assumed in light of the Danish cartoon crisis, Muslims around the world, in majorities greater than 90% in Egypt, Indonesia and Iran, said that they would include free speech as a fundamental guarantee, if they were to draft a new constitution for a new country. When respondents were asked to describe their dreams for the future, we did not hear about waging jihad, but instead we heard about getting a better job, better economic well-being and prosperity and offering a better future to their children. This response was heard among 70% of Indonesians and 54% of Iranians. But Muslims wish to achieve progress within their own religion and culture and to neither be preached to by the West nor forced to adopt Western culture. So while admiring much about the West, they wish to achieve progress through their own culture and in their own way. Despite admiring much about the West, few said adopting Western values would help Muslims progress. Instead, among the statements most frequently associated with the Muslim world was 'attachment to their spiritual and moral values would help progress.' However, this attachment should not be mistaken for a desire to be isolated from the West. In fact 'eager to have better relations with the West' was also among the statements most frequently associated with the Muslim world.

It is a Question of Policy, not Religion

In fact, Muslims do not see the West as monolithic: their perception of different nations falls along policy, not cultural or religious lines. For example, while the United States and the United Kingdom are viewed negatively, views of France and Germany are neutral to positive – in fact, they are viewed as positively as are other Muslim majority countries. For example, while 74% of Egyptians have unfavourable views of the United States and 69% say the same about Britain, only 21% have unfavourable views of France, while 30% express this view of Pakistan. This issue becomes especially clear when we compare the United States to our neighbour to the north: Canada – that is, America without the foreign policy. For example, while 67% of Kuwaitis have unfavourable views of the United States, this percentage for Canada is 3%. Whereas 64% of Malaysians say the United States is 'aggressive', only 1 in 10 associates this quality with France and Germany. Britain fares better than does America, but not by much in some cases. For example, 77% of Lebanese say the United States is aggressive and 45% say the same about Britain, but only 8% assign the same attribute to France and Germany. For many Muslims, this 'aggressive' label is likely reflected in attitudes about the UK and US-led invasion of Iraq, which vast majorities say did more harm than good, including 90% of Egyptians, 87% of Senegalese and even 57% of the Iranians. Muslims clearly see the conflict not as a conflict with Western civilisation as a whole, but instead with specific Western powers based on the negative perceptions of their policies, not their principles.

 ## Muslims' Main Concern is over Western Hypocrisy in the Pursuit of Policy

Many Muslims around the world, while admiring Western values, believe that some Western powers do not live these values in their treatment of Muslims. For example, significant percentages of Muslims around the world do not believe the US is serious about democracy in their regions. This is the view especially in countries where democratic promotion has been the loudest, such as Egypt, where 72% doubt American promises of democratic support and Pakistan, where 55% have this view. Doubting American intentions with regard to democracy is closely tied with the perception that America is a hegemonic neocolonial power that controls the region. More than 65% of Egyptians, Jordanians and Iranians believe that the US will not allow people in their region to fashion their own political future the way they see fit without direct US influence. What Muslims say they admire most about the West, they associate most strongly with the US and the UK: citizen liberties. Yet at the same time, they believe the US is denying Muslims these same rights of self-determination.

To explain the deep gap between America's espoused values of democracy, human rights and self-determination on the one hand, and its perceived treatment of Muslims on the other, Muslims turn to the belief that America and its allies must be hostile toward Islam and regard Muslims as inferior. The idea being that since the perceived way Muslims are treated is so antithetical to admired Western values these same Western powers must simply be singling Muslims out. So, not surprisingly, when we asked Muslims around the world what the West can do to improve relations with the Muslim world, the most frequent responses were for the West to demonstrate more respect for Islam and to regard Muslims as equals, not as inferior. For example, when we asked this question to Lebanese respondents only days after the end of the conflict between Hezbollah and Israel, a war respondent told us they blamed America almost as much as they blamed Israel. Respondents had this to say: 'they [the West] should consider us humans and should end war and be at peace with the Muslim World', and 'the West should treat Muslims equally to improve their relations because they look down upon us.' Other respondents from around the world echoed this sentiment. For example, a respondent from Morocco said: 'The West has to change and moderate their attitudes towards Muslims. They have to not look down on our people.'

Currently Americans Have Little Respect for Muslims

How accurate is this perception? In fact, anti-Muslim sentiment is widespread in the West. For example, Americans were asked how much prejudice they had, if any, against a number of religious groups. While 72% of Americans said they had no prejudice toward Jews, only 34% could say the same about Muslims, and 14% of Americans said they had a 'great deal' of prejudice. It is worth noting, however, that the trend is gradually changing: it went down to 19% in 2007. Other Western views are not much better. The British public is actually the most positive compared to the US, France and Germany, as they are the only one of the four where slightly more people had positive (3 in 10) than negative (2 in 10) opinions of Muslims. At the other end, the German public was at least three times more likely to hold negative (27%) as positive views (7%) of Muslims.

When examining common American perceptions of Muslims, it is not hard to understand where these negative views are coming from. For instance, Gallup found that most Americans believe most Muslims do not believe in gender equality. Gallup found that 72% of Muslims disagreed with this statement: 'The majority of those living in Muslim countries thought men and women should have equal rights.'

How accurate is this perception? Do the majority of those living in Muslim countries think men and women should have equal rights? The answer is yes, they do. In fact, majorities in even some of the most conservative Muslim societies directly refute this assessment: 73% of Saudis, 89% of Iranians and 94% of Indonesians say that men and women should have equal legal rights. Majorities of Muslim men and women in dozens of countries around the world also believe that a woman should have the right to work outside the home in any job for which she is qualified (88% in Indonesia, 72% in Egypt and even 78% in Saudi Arabia), and to vote without interference from family members (87% in Indonesia, 91% in Egypt, 98% in Lebanon).

What about Muslim sympathy for terrorism? Many charge that Islam encourages violence more than other faiths do, but studies show that Muslims around the world are at least as likely as Americans to condemn attacks on civilians. Polls show that 6% of the American public thinks attacks in which civilians are targets are 'completely justified.' In Saudi Arabia, this figure is 4%. In Lebanon and Iran, it is 2%. Moreover, it is politics, not piety, that drives the minority (7% of Muslims) to anti-Americanism at the level of condoning the attacks on the Twin Towers and the Pentagon. Looking across majority-Muslim countries, Gallup found no statistical difference in self-reported religiosity between those who sympathised with the attackers and those who did not. When respondents in select countries were asked in an open-ended question to explain their views of 9/11, those who condemned it cited humanitarian as well as religious reasons. For example, 20% of Kuwaitis who called the attacks 'completely unjustified' explained this position by saying that terrorism was against the teachings of Islam. A respondent in Indonesia went so far as to quote a direct verse from the Qur'an prohibiting killing innocents. On the other hand, not a single respondent who condoned the attacks used the Qur'an as justification. Instead, they relied on political rationalisations, calling the US an imperialist power or accusing it of wanting to control the world. If most Muslims truly reject terrorism, why does it continue to flourish in Muslim countries? In fact, when asked what they admired least about the Muslim world, respondents in many countries talked about fanaticism and extremism even more frequently than Americans who responded to the same question did. Many Muslims also said that their greatest fear was being a victim of a terrorist attack. What these results indicate is that terrorism is much like other violent crime. Violent crimes occur throughout US cities, but that is no indication of Americans' general acceptance of murder or assault. Likewise, continued terrorist violence is not proof that Muslims tolerate it. Indeed, they are its primary victims.

Still, the average American and European cannot be blamed for these misperceptions. Media-content analyses show that the majority of US, UK and German TV news coverage of Islam is sharply negative. People are bombarded every day with stories about Muslims and majority-Muslim countries in which vocal extremists drive perceptions. In the end, the current conflict between the West and the Muslim world is not inevitable. It is about policy, not a clash between religions or principles. Polls found that Lebanese hold Christians and Muslims in high regard (more than 90% hold favourable opinions of each)[2] despite a decades-long civil war in Lebanon fought roughly along confessional lines. Today, less than a generation after the civil rights struggle, a majority of blacks and whites in America say relations between their groups are good.[3] In 1956, only 4% of Americans said they approved of a marriage between blacks and whites. Today that number is 80%. President Obama was born at a time when his parents' marriage was illegal in Virginia. He was the first Democratic candidate in decades to win Virginia, and of course went on to win the 2008 election. These hopeful examples underscore the possibility of improving relations between groups, even those whose conflicts lasted centuries, and the relative speed by which this is possible. Rather than allow extremists on either side to dictate how we discuss Islam and the West, we need to listen carefully to the voices of ordinary people and thus let facts, not fear, shape our global engagement.

Notes

1   John Esposito & Dalia Mogahed's, *Who Speaks for Islam? What a billion Muslims really think, Based on Gallup's World Poll – the largest study of its kind* (New York: Gallup Press; 2007)
2   Pew Poll May 2006.
3   Gallup Poll June 2006.

Islam Studies, Foreign Policy and the Muslim World: From Bush to Obama

John Esposito

What I want to talk about first is the background for my final set of comments about the academy and the role of academics. So, 'where are we, what do we need to be doing and what about the role of academics?'

President Bush, as we all know, right after 9/11 and throughout his presidency always distinguished between Islam and extremism. At the end of the day, his policies, in fact, did not do that. If anything, the Bush administration's policies fed the belief in many parts of the Muslim world that the war on global terrorism was a war against the Islam and the Muslim world. It confirmed the concern of a colleague, a first-grade academic and an Islamic activist in Egypt: 'Of course you will want to go after Bin Laden and go into Afghanistan, but we wonder whether this is the beginning or the end'. I emailed her back and said 'what do you mean by that?', and she wrote back and said 'will this become an excuse for America to redraw the map of the Middle-East and the Muslim world?'.

When you look at the trajectory of the Bush/Blair/Cheney legacy and its approach, it tended to play into that belief. Before America had just about gone into Afghanistan, we began to talk about second frontiers and to speculate on everything from Somalia to the Philippines. In the middle of a Fox TV programme interview right after the president and the head of the CIA and the FBI were interviewed live, in which I was talking about the need of our approach to the Muslim world to be focused and discriminating, the interviewer interrupted me and said: 'Did you hear him?! Did you hear what the president said? Are you deaf? We have a global threat here. We [the interviewer's opinion] should go into all 56 of their countries, if we want'.

Then the Bush administration spoke of an axis of evil; the axis-of-evil countries were overwhelmingly Muslim with the exception of North-Korea. For the Muslim countries the administration and many in Congress talked or threatened, when convenient, military action. In contrast, for North-Korea, a country that in fact has nuclear capability and demonstrates it publicly, the US always talked about the ability to use diplomacy. This was followed by the invasion of Iraq, in which the excuse for the invasion went from weapons of mass destruction and when none were discovered, to the liberation of Iraq and the promotion of democracy. Shortly after advocating the promotion of democracy, we invaded and occupied Iraq. And we did it with the worst possible intelligence, thinking that it was going to be an easy undertaking, that we would simply be welcomed by the Iraqis.

US policies in the first two years after 9/11 convinced many that it was a neocolonial power, that is, the US-UK approach was to define the form of government and determine Iraq's new leader Ahmad Chelabi. We felt free to say – and this is a phrase that we often use both in America and in Europe when we deal with countries, particularly in the Muslim world – 'we won't allow it' with that clear implication that we have that power and authority. And indeed much of the approach and rhetoric was driven by the vision of a New American century, informed by a report and plan written by neocons many years before George W. Bush became president (which you can look up on the internet). Many of the neocons who had drawn up their vision of the New American century, like Paul Wolfowitz (Assistant Secretary of Defence) and others, were responsible for Bush's foreign policy. And certainly the extent to which this was the case even at the end of the Bush presidency – even though the rhetoric of Bush's policy did shift in the second period – could be seen in the American response to Gaza and to Lebanon during the Israeli invasions. It fed that notion of an America that is neocolonial and biased, not even-handed.

Bush's domestic policy led to the erosion of civil liberties in America – an issue that Europe itself faces. Aggressive policies, which are good in their concern for national security to fight terrorism, resulted in indiscriminate profiling, arrest and detentions without hard evidence. A conservative estimate of more than 6,000 people were arrested in America shortly after 9/11 and only a handful ever found guilty of anything. The situation was compounded internationally by Abu Ghraib, Guantamo, extraordinary rendition, water boarding and the list goes on.

The Obama administration is now dealing with that Bush legacy. What does that mean for Americans and Europeans? The legacy of the Bush/ Blair era compromised the principles and values, *our* principles and values in the name of security. Obama acknowledges the departure, if you look at his inaugural address, in a number of ways and said something which I think is especially important: power alone cannot protect us nor does it entitle us to do as we please. He said what many believed was taking place: a unilateral rather than a multilateral approach, a belief that we had the power, the military power to do what we wanted, not only in the region, but when we felt comfortable to say to our European allies: 'This is what we were going to do, we invite you to come along, but if you choose not to or if you have objections, we will do it ourselves'.

Future relations between the West and the Muslim world will require a joint effort, a process of constructive engagement, listening not just telling, dialogue, self-criticism and change. How does this play out? Who needs to do what? Mainstream Muslims worldwide will need to address more aggressively, even more aggressively, the threat to Islam from religious extremists. This is happening, but it remains a significant problem for Muslim communities. On the other hand, Muslim governments in particular, many of whom rely on authoritarian rule and security forces for their legitimacy and not on elections, and continue to want to go that way, will need reform. A number of them actually use the trappings of democracy and civil society to make it look like they are opening up. So in Egypt, what do we have? A seeming proliferation of NGOs, but they are government-regulated non-governmental organisations, a contradiction in terms. In Jordan, they are called 'royal NGOs'. These governments need to either move, or, if they do not want to move in that direction which is often the case, be pushed by their Western allies, through a carrot and stick approach, to open up their political systems to build and strengthen civil society; to discriminate between free speech and mainstream opposition and violent extremists and terrorists. In fact, post-9/11 most of these governments, as does even the government of India on occasion and certainly the government of Israel, use the threat of terrorism to repress not only terrorists, but any and all significant opposition.

Western governments and policymakers, religious leaders and the media and the general public are challenged to play both critical and constructive roles, building or rebuilding the new way forward. It has to be a joint partnership that emphasises our shared beliefs, values and interests. To see the beliefs and values side, all you need to do is look at the Gallup World Poll and other polls that Gallup has done in Europe. To see that there is hard evidence for showing that despite differences, there is much that we share in common; that many of the aspirations that Muslims globally have are shared by non-Muslims. The fact is that many of us who are experts and pseudo-experts on this part of the world, often until recently could not with any credibility say that we had massive data to back up what we were saying. No matter how much I travel around the Muslim world, no matter how many people I know, how many people can I actually get to meet? How many situations do I get to know in depth? We can now get beyond that 'battle of the experts'; we now know what mainstream Muslims as well as those who are politically radicalised really think rather than simply relying on an individual or individuals.

Today, we need in particular to re-examine our foreign policies and in time also our domestic policies. From the US point of view, and also Europe's, there needs to be a willingness to press our Muslim allies, in many cases our long-standing Muslim allies, so-called democratic governments like Tunisia where the president can win by 99.91% of the vote (and in a bad year by only 95%, and when it is really liberal 92% and often with no opposition). Egypt, where the government controls the existence of political parties, how they operate, who runs for office and has a president who was the vice-president of Anwar Sadat. He has avoided appointing a vice-president during his presidency, because this could be divisive. You only have to look at recent Egyptian elections (2005) in which there was virtually no significant opposition. The one person Hosni Mubarak had in opposition was arrested, tried, released, allowed to run and afterwards he was rearrested, found guilty, sentenced, I think, to five years in prison.[1] We (Western governments) need to have a short- and long-term policy. We have to figure out a way to operate at times with governments that we may not be thrilled about, but we need a long-term policy on how we are going to open up those societies.

Otherwise, ten years from now, we will be looking at the same conditions and drawing the conclusion that it must be something about Arab and Muslim religion or culture that makes them that way. The temptation then, as it is now, will be to seek easy justification to explain away anti-Americanism or anti-Westernism as simply irrationality, ingratitude, clash of civilisations, a hate of our way of life.

The extremists aside, the bulk of criticism and contempt, for example, of US policy, comes from those who judge by our admirable principles and values. The Gallup World Poll shows that many in the Muslim world admire our principles and values. That is why many want to come and study in America, many decide to come. After 9/11 people said they hated us for who we are. But then there was the question, 'why are they still queuing up to get visas, why do they still want to come here?' In fact, the criticism of the US and the West in general is that we promote self-determination, democracy and human rights but not in the Muslim world. A senior Bush administration official, Ambassador Richard Haass, admitted that when it came to the promotion of democracy in the Muslim world, every president, democrat or republican, including George W. Bush in his first term, practised 'democratic exceptionalism'. We chose not to promote democracy and human rights in that part of the world. As the Gallup World Poll indicates, despite significant differences, regardless of cultural differences, most people in the world share a common civilisation – one that values life, family, education, technology, peace, social justice, freedom and political participation.

The final point here, as I move to the role of academia is a corrected approach to public diplomacy, winning hearts and minds. Too often, during the Bush administration, public diplomacy was reduced to public relations (the need to communicate more, exchange programmes, education etc.). The PR approach does not work, because the cause of the problem is not simply that they do not know us – many of the people who have a problem with our policy know us well; they are military, academics, business people, government bureaucrats, many of whom have studied in the West. But, they have a problem with American foreign policy and American-European foreign policy at times, when it comes down to the way in which we handle the promotion of democracy and elections, for example, the way we (America and Europe) reacted when Hamas was elected in free and fair elections, the kinds of sanctions and conditions that we alongside Israel put in place, which have devastated the people and the land.

So then, looking at our foreign policy and the implications, we need a more data-driven public diplomacy that looks at foreign policy in terms of what we really know when we listen to the voices of the mainstream majority. We need to emphasise diplomacy, educational, technological, economic and military assistance. President Obama and some leaders in Europe now advocate this verbally, if not always in reality. But please remember that both Bush and Blair said, at the time of the invasions of Afghanistan and Iraq, that there would be a massive infusion of economic and educational aid. That simply never occurred. And if the situation becomes as insecure as it has become in Afghanistan, then it becomes hard to even do that. Without security, how do you build schools? Remember what Admiral Mike Mullen, the Chairman of the Joint Chiefs of Staff, said in a recent article. In a critique of US government, he emphasized strategic communications efforts. 'To put it simply,' he said, 'we need to worry a lot less about how to communicate our actions, but much more about what our actions communicate'.

We have the need for a new paradigm. We need to go beyond the smokescreens, stereotypes, disinformation and lies created by neocons, anti-immigrant ideologies and Islamophobic experts, who foster and play on fear and prejudice. We need to deal with the realities of autocratic rulers/allies. We need to emphasise, again, educational, technological support, not massive military support. Military aid, weapons and training are often not used by regimes for external security, to defend their countries, but for internal security to control and crush any and all opposition. That is why in many authoritarian countries American military presence, and particularly our training and weapons, are so resented. When, for example, you have people in Lebanon and Gaza being fired upon – and this is not to legitimate everything that Hamas and Hezbollah did – by the Israeli military with American helicopter-ships and American weapons: that angers and undermines credibility. We need to marginalise and de-legitimise terrorists, realising that to do so requires foreign-policy reform. We need to reach out and work more with the mainstream majority in the Muslim world in partnership to marginalise the terrorists. We need to avoid feeding the arguments that extremists and terrorists make. The big fear of many in the Arab and Muslim world is Western interference, intervention, or occupation; not economic aid – majorities of Muslims want economic aid, technological aid, educational aid, who would not? But a big fear of many is interven-tion and dependency. Is there a reason for that? If you look at recent history, there is a reason for concern.

Policymakers have to balance their bias towards authoritarian allies with a more even-handed response to both Islamic and secular opposi-tion and reform movements. We need to realise and follow the maxim: 'pay me now or pay me later'. We need to address these issues now, or we will reap what we sow. President Obama's challenge in pursuing both a short- and long-term strategy in Palestine-Israel entails the sup-port for the existence and security of the state of Israel, but also the equal support for the creation of a secure and economically supported Palestinian state. Now! Not five years from now or ten years from now. It means working with leaders on both sides, all leaders, however much both sides have leaders that may not be the best leaders to achieve any-thing: Mahmud Abbas and Hamas, Benjamin Netanyahu and Avigdor Lieberman. We cannot just say 'we'll go with Abbas', who does not en-joy widespread support, and not deal with Hamas which was democratically elected. So we need to be very realistic and balanced, we need to condemn, in no uncertain terms, acts of illegitimate violence and terror committed by the Israeli military just as we have condemned those acts committed by Palestinians. We need to get beyond the Israel lobby; we need to get beyond the hard-line Christian Zionists and their influence on the US Congress.

Now let us turn to the academy, what do we do? (I was asked to address this issue in terms not only of my knowledge but also of my experience so bear with the self-reference and use of anecdotes). I had an interest-ing set of interviews today with some very good journalists, who repeated what I have often heard from some other journalists. Things like 'you know, people in our society ask: where are the moderates, where are the mainstream Muslims, why are they not speaking out?'. This is what I call one of the perennial questions, demonstrating that we have a severe learning curve. Since 9/12, the day after 9/11, while there were extremists who applauded, we know from the Gallup poll that majorities of Muslims deplored 9/11. And more importantly, you do not need that data; all you need to do is look at statements by major Muslim leaders. But you say 'I don't hear them, I don't see them'. I have often heard that question from the media and then I say 'they exist and I can send you the websites'. Then, who is the problem? If you follow the media but do not see them and you do not hear them, whose fault is it? Is it their fault? Is it the media that tends to emphasise explosive headline events? As Jon Meachem, editor of *Newsweek*, stated in a public session, 'the media is a business obviously concerned with sales; and what sells, is conflict or conflictual discourse and issues.'

Prior to the Iranian revolution, the role of religion in international affairs and knowledge of Islam and the Muslim world were not serious concerns of government, academia and the general public. Thus, diplomats were not trained to look at the role of religion and culture in politics. Governments did not expect them to report on it. This attitude was caused in large part by the prevailing theory of modernisation and development that for a nation and its peoples to become modern required a process of secularisation and Westernisation. Rather than today's notion of multiple modernities, the belief was that there was only one model, one modernity and one norm for what it meant to be modern. Thus, there was no field of religion in international affairs. Social scientists saw religion as either part of the past – so you might look at it to understand the past, as part of history – or as part of the past in the sense of being an obstacle to change, something that with modernisation would become peripheral. After so many years of neglect, that is why the Social Science Research Council has major projects now, bringing together a group of us to talk about 'how do we understand the role of religion in a secular society? How do we reconfigure the field? Let alone, how do we teach it?' I was hired at Georgetown University in 1993, the oldest school of international affairs in the world, and yet I was the first professor of religion in international affairs. It was not until years later that we introduced a concentration in politics and culture, one of the most popular courses today.

Now, a second factor is bias. People who were trained in Islam and Islamic studies, in general, were trained in the old days to be orientalists with language and texts, not contexts. You could be a leading expert on Sufism (Islamic mysticism) and never leave the UK, never have put your foot down in a Muslim country, never have visited a major Sufi league. When I wrote an introduction to Islam, people said 'why are you doing that, there are already two or three of them out there'. This was incredible, the two and three texts were more than twenty years old, written by great scholars who knew how to write for graduate students, but not for non-specialists, undergraduates and the general public. In all those books, the shortest chapter was the modern period, the last chapter which covered the entire nineteenth and twentieth century in 15 or 20 pages.

So where were we in terms of the modern Islamic world? Only ten years ago I met with a woman who was going to be very prominent in the field. She was concerned because she was trained as an orientalist, but was also interested in a lot of contemporary stuff. But she was advised by her friends, 'don't go into the contemporary stuff, that is newspaper stuff, you will never have a career'. But you will have better sales (...) anyway, that is a different matter. What I am trying to say is 'remember the backgrounds, remember that the ivory tower is viewed as the ivory tower'. We are sort of seen not only by ourselves as being above that dirty little area called government, but also not wanting to be compromised by it, be used by it, not wanting to be seen as a kind of embodiment of colonialism or the CIA.

When I wrote my introduction, I wrote about texts in a context. People kept saying 'how did your methodology develop?'. I did not know I had a specific or special methodology; I was simply trying to describe Islam as a faith and way of life today. Nobody trained me in that methodology. When I was first asked to meet with government and advise them, I went to a reception at the annual meeting of the American Academy of Religion hoping to meet Wilfred Cantwell Smith, a prominent scholar of Islam. How do I get the conversation going? I said, 'I have been asked by the government to advise them' and he said, 'of course you won't; I mean, we, academics don't do that' and Wilfred was very serious. I was really conflicted. After the United States tried to kill Kaddafi and the bombing of Libya, Cantwell Smith found my phone number, called me up and said, 'I changed my mind, you need to talk to your government and I'll talk to the Canadian government'.

What academics realised was that we had something to contribute – even if at times government did not appreciate it. And we needed to do that. We could not just write our articles, while complaining that governments were getting it wrong; we could not just hold forth in front of an audience. But that was relatively new and we always had the concern, especially because people in the region were often suspicious and would ask, 'do you have any connection to the government? Are you CIA?'

The reality of it is that we have an opportunity now and an obligation as academics to be, what I call, public intellectuals, not just academics. What does that mean? What are the risks, what are the successes? What can we do? Those of us who write on areas that are relevant and important for policy decision making need to seek venues that make our ideas and advice accessible. We can choose not to. I have no problem with colleagues who are very specialised and who make incredible contributions, but at the end of the day write for a very small group of other like-minded people. But if you want to have an impact, you have to write that, plus write that for broader audiences. You have to be able to speak to broader audiences. You have to be able to speak to policymakers, government agencies, to general audiences, to corporate leaders, etc.

There is a great need and demand today by governments and corporations for our knowledge and experience because people have realised more and more – this is where Huntington was right – that after the fall of the Soviet Union, global politics has been driven in large part by a resurgence of ethnic, tribal and religious nationalism and thus religion, politics and culture are often integrally related. We have seen this not only in the Muslim world, but in the former Yugoslavia, India in conflicts between Hindus, Muslims and Christians, Sri Lanka, and Israel.

The need was reflected during the first term of George W. Bush, when fairly senior level people at the Justice Department and Homeland Security asked me to speak at and help organise an informal set of luncheon talks by academic experts on Muslim-West relations. He said: 'The reasons why we want to have these luncheons is that we realised we are so busy making policy that we have no time to learn anything about the people in the areas that we are making policy about.' If you are making policies about Muslim citizens in your country or Muslim citizens coming from other countries and if most of the people who are doing this, do not know the context, you have a problem.

What does it mean for those of us that choose to get involved? On the one hand, you can have influence – sometimes you do not realise it. But during the first Bush (George Herbert Walker Bush) presidency, his assistant secretary of state, Edward Djerejian, gave the first major speech on American policy and Islam.[2] He talked about the fact that the US had no problem with the Islam and Muslims or with Islamic secular movements participating in politics, as long as they did not believe in 'one man, one vote, one time etc.'. That policy was influenced by a number of us who were engaged in regular conversations and meetings with State Department officials who advised Djerejian.

Sometimes the influence can be more indirect such as when we are asked by professionals in US and foreign government agencies who are restricted by the policies of agency heads or officials with whom they disagree, to speak on topics on which our position is antithetical to that of their government. As I have been told: 'We need you to say some of the things that we believe, we then write a report on the conference and submit... you reinforce what we say as well as bring another dimension.' It would have been unthinkable in the past for government to consult academics on the role of religion in Muslim politics and foreign policy and indeed many academics as a matter of policy avoided speaking to government officials.

The fact that I, like others, would be asked today to advise the British Foreign Secretary David Miliband on his major address on the Middle East or comment on the text of Barack Obama's Cairo speech is a sign of the times. Academics have an opportunity to make that policy shift, but only if they can frame what they know in a way that is clear and policy relevant. Only if it resonates with the issues policymakers face and they see that connection. Seeing that connection has to do with both the way we frame what we know, communicate clearly and persuasively what we know without burying them. The first consultation I did many years ago was a three-hour presentation for government people. When asked afterwards, 'can you come back?', I said 'why are you asking me? You had so and so last year, one of the great names in the field.' He responded that they had had him for six hours but the problem was that he started with the birth of the Prophet Muhammad and it had taken them four hours to get to the current situation. Having spent many years teaching undergraduates and speaking to public audiences, I had started with the contemporary situation and then showed how past history was relevant. So, we need to speak in a style and language that is accessible and cut to the chase rather than constantly qualifying what we say with – 'on the one hand, on the other...': that is the kiss of death! A very senior Iranian scholar had resented the fact that she was never invited to the State Department. When she finally did get an invitation. I asked her, 'how did it go?' she said, 'it went fine'. I called a friend at State who responded, 'it didn't go fine ... she came in – she is a historian – she presented the history of Iran, we sat through the whole thing. When we asked, 'what do you think we should do, where should we go with this?' she said, 'that is not my job, that is yours'.

There are many other ways in which we can have impact and influence. I have gone out of my way to produce the major reference works for Oxford University Press. That sounds very academic, but major reference works over time are used to train students, scholars and people in the media consult them. We also have Oxford Islamic Studies Online, which makes references works, books, documents, maps and art readily available on the internet. We can produce books, DVDs and other materials that speak to audiences beyond a small group of specialists and be used in training sessions for government, military, corporate, church and media leaders.

Let me end with the other side. I learned years ago that in academia our philosophy is that if you stick your head up, we will shoot it off. We are not trained to work as a team. Many, if not most academics, especially in Islamic studies, live in their little disciplinary modules. Many in the field of Islamic studies, Oriental studies and history have been trained in the past to think of textual studies and history as real scholarship and not value writing on the contemporary period and for broader audiences or consulting with government. For many, signing public statements of concern take the place of addressing in a more sustained fashion public issues. Fortunately, the times are changing. However, there are costs for those who choose to be academics and public intellectuals. You have to learn to multitask and are often faced with an even more time-consuming lifestyle. Also, when you step out in public, you can become a lightning rod. If some people do not like what you say, post-9/11 as you know, you end up in a book called 'The 101 Most Dangerous Professors' or attacked (not just commented on or argued with) in far-right and Islamophobic publications and websites.

We live today in a highly politicised world, in highly polarised societies in Europe and America. It is compounded by a media dominated by explosive headlines, shout-television that emphasises confrontation and conflict. A culture war exists, led by far-right neocons and the hardline Christian Zionist right. And it plays out not only in the media, but in the academy and among experts and pseudo-experts of conflict and terrorism. This battle of experts, political commentators and politicians can only be countered by a more data-driven analysis that reflects the views of the vast majority of Muslims and not just the extremists. We now get more of that data from the Gallup World Poll, Pew and others. At the same time, we need more academics to step out as public intellectuals. That means that you have to be willing to take risks. But too often, too many of us have not been willing to speak out. Look at some of the major departments in Europe and America with top specialists, how many of them or, more accurately, how few of them spoke out when it came to the US/UK-led invasion and occupation of Iraq, or the Israeli invasions in Gaza and Lebanon? Certainly nowhere near the number you would expect. Why? Because most of us, quite understandably, do not like to be criticised, attacked or disliked. Most of us do not like hate-mail or even death threats. I am not saying that to those of you who want to step out in the field, you will be subject to all of this. But if we want to move forward in our societies, we have to realise that we live in an increasingly polarised world and in societies where too often Islam and mainstream Muslims are judged by the rhetoric and actions of an extremist minority.

Today, in international politics as well as domestic politics, we have a chance to turn things around, we have a new American administration; we have a president who has a vision, but it is not clear whether that president will be able to deliver, given the magnitude of the problems he has inherited from the Bush administration and our own domestic political situation. It is going to depend a lot on how much support he is going to get from within the United States, as well as how the European Union and European countries respond. If Europe and the US respond in the way that they have in the past when it comes to policy in the Middle-East and in the Palestine and Israeli conflict, and if they do not address more forcefully the influence of far-right anti-immigrant politics, the growth of Islamophobia and the erosion of civil liberties in their domestic situation, then while things may get better long-term, the situation will get worse short-term.

Note

1   The time of writing of this piece was autumn 2009, before the start of the 'Arab Spring' and the overthrow of Zine El Abidine Ben Ali and Hosni Mubarak.
2   Meridian House Speech, Washington DC, 4 June 1992.

About the Authors

Wendy Asbeek-Brusse

Wendy Asbeek Brusse has been Director of the Scientific Council for Government Policy for the Netherlands (WRR) since 2009. Before this appointment she held a position at the Dutch Ministry of Housing, Spatial Planning and Environment as Deputy Head of Division and Senior Policy Advisor in the Division for Integration and Communities. From 1998 to 2007, she was a Senior Research Fellow at the WRR, involved in, among others, the publication of the reports *Europe in the Netherlands* (2007), *Dynamism in Islamic Activism* (2006), *The European Union, Turkey and Islam* (2004) and *Towards a Pan-European Union* (2001). Asbeek Brusse studied history at the Free University in Amsterdam and obtained her PhD in 1991. She has taught at the universities of Groningen and Leiden.

Maurits Berger

Maurits Berger is Professor of Islam in the Contemporary Western World at the Faculty of Humanities and the Institute of Theology of Leiden University. He holds the 'Sultan of Oman Chair for Oriental Studies'. Berger is an Arabist and a jurist. He obtained his PhD from the University of Amsterdam on Islamic family law in Egypt. Previously he worked as a solicitor and as a journalist and researcher in Cairo and Damascus. Next to his professorship he continues to be a researcher connected to the Clingendael Institute in The Hague. His research interests concern the relationship between the Islam and law, specifically the role of sharia in the West. He also looks at political Islam and the freedom of religion. Berger is a member of the steering group of LUCIS.

Léon Buskens

Léon Buskens is Professor of Law and Culture in Islamic Societies at the Faculty of Humanities as well as the Law Faculty, notably at its Van Vollenhoven Institute for Law, Governance and Development. Buskens studied cultural anthropology at the University of Nijmegen, as well as Arabic language and culture, Moroccan Arabic and Islamology. In 1993, he obtained his PhD from the Faculty of Law of Leiden University on

'Islamic Law and Family Relations in Morocco'. Since 1991, Buskens
has been teaching courses on Islamic law and anthropology of the
Middle-East. Between 1998 and 2008, he occupied the chair 'Law and
Culture of the Islam' at the Faculty of Law of Utrecht University.
Buskens' research interests concern Islamic and customary law, with
specific focus on Morocco, and the anthropology of the Muslim world.
Buskens is chair of the steering group of LUCIS.

Job Cohen

Since 2010, Job Cohen has been the leader of the Dutch Labour Party
(Partij van de Arbeid – PvdA) and member of the House of
Representatives, where he is also the parliamentary group leader of the
Labour Party. He obtained his Master of Law at the University of
Groningen (1971) and his PhD at Leiden University (1981). In 1983, he
became a law professor of methods and techniques. In 1991, he was appointed *rector magnificus* at Maastricht University. As a member of the
Labour Party, Cohen held several political positions and offices over the
years. He was State Secretary for Education and Sciences (1993-1994),
member of and parliamentary group leader in the Senate (1995-1998)
and State Secretary for Justice (1998-2001). The contribution included
in this book is an adaptation of a speech he gave during his office as
Mayor of Amsterdam (2001-2010), when he was awarded 'Best Mayor
in the Netherlands in 25 years' by the Ministry of Interior in 2005,
Hero of Europe by *Time Magazine* in 2005 and the second-best World
Mayor Award in 2006.

Nikolaos van Dam

Nikolaos van Dam served as Ambassador of the Netherlands to
Indonesia (2005-2010), Germany (1999-2005), Turkey (1996-1999),
Egypt (1991-1996) and Iraq (1988-1991). He studied Arabic and
Political & Social Sciences at the University of Amsterdam, and served
most of his academic and diplomatic career in the Arab world, also cov-
ering Libya, Lebanon, Jordan and the Palestinian Occupied Territories.
He has published widely with the fourth edition of *The Struggle for
Power in Syria: Politics and Society under Asad and the Ba'th Party*
(London & New York: I.B. Tauris; 2011) having just appeared.

John Esposito

John Esposito is University Professor, Professor of Religion and
International Affairs and Professor of Islamic Studies at Georgetown
University, USA. He is the Founding Director of the Prince Alwaleed
Bin Talal Center for Muslim-Christian Understanding in the Walsh
School of Foreign Service. At the College of the Holy Cross, he was
Loyola Professor of Middle East Studies, Chair of the Department of

Religious Studies and Director of the Center for International Studies. As a consultant to the Department of State as well as to corporations, universities, and the media worldwide, Esposito specialises in Islam, political Islam and the impact of Islamic movements from North Africa to Southeast Asia. He has published numerous books and articles, and was the Editor-in-Chief of the 4-volume *Oxford Encyclopedia of the Modern Islamic World, The Oxford History of Islam* and *The Oxford Dictionary of Islam and The Islamic World: Past and Present*. He is co-author of the book *Who Speaks for Islam? What a Billion Muslims Really Think* (New York: Gallup Press; 2007).

Jaap de Hoop Scheffer
Jaap de Hoop Scheffer held the office of NATO Secretary General between 2004 and 2009. He studied law at Leiden University, graduating in 1974. Previous to his appointment at the NATO, he was the Dutch Minister of Foreign Affairs, member and leader of the Christian Democratic Party (CDA) in the House of Representatives. As a diplomat he served a.o. at the Dutch Embassy in Accra (Ghana) and at the Permanent Representation of the NATO in Brussels. Since 2009, De Hoop Scheffer holds the Pieter Kooijmans chair in peace, justice and security at Leiden University, teaching courses in international politics and contemporary diplomacy.

Hannah Mason
Hannah Mason has been a research assistant to Jan Michiel Otto since 2009. In this position she has also edited and translated several books and articles for the Van Vollenhoven Institute, the Leiden University Centre for the Study of Islam and Society (LUCIS), the Netherlands Interuniversity School for Islamic Studies (NISIS) and the Islam Research Programme (IRP). In the mean time, she is preparing a comparative research project on sexual and reproductive health (rights) with a focus on policy and legislation regarding female genital mutilation in the Middle East and Africa. She holds a MA (University of Oxford) and a MSc (University of Amsterdam). She previously (2005-2008) worked at Advisory of a UK-based political consultancy, where she managed several projects following socio-economic and political trends and developments in areas including Sub-Saharan Africa, Iran, the Gulf and Central Asia. She has been a freelance contributor to the Economist Intelligence Unit (UK) since 2008.

Dalia Mogahed
Dalia Mogahed is Senior Analyst at Gallup and Executive Director of the Gallup Center for Muslim Studies. She is co-author of the book *Who Speaks for Islam? What a Billion Muslims Really Think* (New York:

Gallup Press; 2007). Mogahed provides leadership, strategic direction and consultation on the collection and analysis of Gallup's unprecedented surveys representing the opinions of more than 1 billion Muslims worldwide. She also directs the Muslim-West Facts Initiative (www.muslimwestfacts.com), through which Gallup, in collaboration with the Coexist Foundation, is disseminating the findings of the Gallup World Poll to key opinion leaders in the Muslim World and the West. In 2009, she was appointed Special Advisor to the Obama Administration in the role of one of the 25 consultants of the 'Office of Religious Partnerships'.

Jan Michiel Otto

Jan Michiel Otto has been Professor of Law and Governance in Developing Countries at Leiden University since 1998. He also is Director of the Van Vollenhoven Institute for Law, Governance and Development, which forms part of the Leiden Law School. He graduated in law and governance at Leiden University and occupied several positions, including at the Ministry of Foreign Affairs and various academic institutions. He spent a considerable amount of time in Egypt and Indonesia carrying out fieldwork and published on a range of issues concerning law and governance in Asia, Africa and the Middle East. This includes the recent *Sharia incorporated* (2010), comparing the relationships between sharia and national law in twelve Muslims countries. Jan Michiel Otto is a member of the steering group of LUCIS.

Petra Sijpesteijn

Petra Sijpesteijn is Professor of Arabic Language and Culture at Leiden University. Having completed her degree in ancient history in 1998, she spent a year at Cornell University, USA. In 2004, she obtained her PhD from Princeton University, USA, on the topic of Arabic papyri. Next she spent three years as a junior research fellow at Christ Church College, University of Oxford, UK. Between 2007 and 2008, she was connected to the 'Institut de Recherche et d'Histoire des Textes', which forms part of the 'Centre National de la Recherche Scientifique' in Paris. Petra Sijpesteijn specialises in the study of Arabic papyri. She is Director and one of the founding members of the International Society for Arabic Papyrology. Her research focuses on the early development of the Islam and its impact on Mediterranean societies and cultures, the relationship between the Islam and already existing cultures and structures, and the continuous interaction between Islamic and non-Islamic societies. Petra Sijpesteijn is a member of the steering group of LUCIS.